THE
FASHION
SWITCH

THE NEW RULES OF THE
FASHION BUSINESS

JOANNE YULAN JONG

RETHINK PRESS

First published in Great Britain 2017 by Rethink
Press (www.rethinkpress.com)

© Copyright Joanne Yulan Jong

Cover image © François Goizé (www.francoisgoize.com)

Contents

I dedicate this book to passionate entrepreneurs who strive to do something different.

I hope that this book inspires you to change the way you think about creativity today.

"This book combines a deep wealth of knowledge from fashion experts and legends alike, as well as the author's own impressive industry experience, to provide a blueprint for creative entrepreneurs in this rapidly evolving digital age. The Fashion Switch is an easy, approachable read complete with personal experiences and case studies that offer practical insight into Joanne's thoughtful and effective methodology. Coupled with thought-provoking exercises, this is a must read for those wading into the churning waters of today's fashion industry."

Marty Wikstrom, Founder, Atelier Fund and Corporate Director

"This is a great read. Joanne has written an indispensable bible, a must read for all designers, whether starting out or years into the game. Joanne generously shares her wealth of experience as a designer for Armani and Missoni and then as an independent brand in her own right, giving a unique insight into how the fashion industry works and how to navigate your way through it most effectively. There's so much fantastic advice in this book, something to learn on every page. I'll certainly be recommending it to people."

Tamsin Blanchard, Fashion Writer and Editor

"The Fashion Switch provides an incredibly insightful view of recent dramatic changes in the fashion industry. It was a relief and a joy to read Joanne's proposals for how to excel in the midst of such flux. The ALIGN framework is a refreshingly sensible method for boiling down and tackling the myriad of challenges facing independent fashion businesses. Joanne empowers her readers to fix the nuts and bolts, tying together our left and right brains, in order to emerge with a healthy, sustainable and functional business model as well as a more differentiated brand and product offering. I would wholeheartedly recommend The Fashion Switch for anyone starting or building a brand."

Sara Madderson, Founder and Director, Madderson London

"*Joanne describes how classic fashion businesses have succeeded to date, through core principles and processes such as a solid financial understanding. She also reveals the current disruptors: digital transformation, the impact of innovation and consumer behaviour on evolving business models, in which customers are centre-stage and purpose becomes an essential component of the value chain.*"

Michelle De Conto, Business Development Adviser, British Fashion Council

"*This is the right book at the right time for an industry facing massive disruption and in search of guidance. Based on decades of industry insight, Joanne uses her outstanding creativity and analytical skills to consolidate a wide range of information. This provides not only a comprehensive overview of how the industry thinks and what the drivers of change are, but also a toolbox to improve your own business decisions. And, it's fun to read and clearly addressed to the creative business minds in this amazing industry. Truly enriching!*"

Thomas Johann Lorenz, Director Business Development Premium Group, Founder Premium Group Digital

"*When I founded Orlebar Brown I had no experience of fashion. People were very generous with their advice, but the tools available were either too simplistic or too complicated. Like many others, I had to learn it all myself. Joanne, with her wealth of experience, explains the fashion business in a clear and succinct way including its challenges and opportunities which enables any potential founder or start up to actually see a way in, provides a framework and makes it all seem possible. This is an invaluable and book for anyone running a fashion business in today's world.*"

Adam Brown, Founder and Creative Director, Orlebar Brown

"*The Fashion Switch is an inspiring book on many levels. I connected immediately with Joanne's thinking not only about the fashion business as a whole, but more around how she clarifies the mindset of successful brands. Her rigorous and systemised approach to reconnect owners to their businesses, and to articulate their meaning and purpose, is invaluable. That blend of thinking like an entrepreneur but striving to deliver the best, creatively and through product, is a winning formula in today's challenging times. Brilliant.*"

Nick Falkingham, Founder, Pure Collection

INTRODUCTION

Did you hear that click?

Something snapped, something changed. It came quietly, crept up on us all. Digital hit the fashion business and shattered it into a billion fragments.

Back in the 1990s, when I was working with Giorgio Armani in Milan, he used to tell me that someone like him, with no formal training, would never again have the opportunity to become a designer. At that time, the big production companies such as GFT, Marzotto, and Miroglio dominated the Italian luxury fashion business. These corporate companies, with their finely tuned systems and rules, had made it difficult for smaller brands to emerge.

The fashion powerhouses were fiercely protective of their market, producing numerous collections, season after season – main lines, diffusion ranges and licenced collections. Journalists from the same magazines were invited to the fashion shows each season. The brands paid for pages of advertising, and in return the journalists gushed about them, writing column inches about the same designers. Loyal stay-fast clients would rush to buy their clothes from the new collection at the same time every year. Happy days.

Then came that click.

It was the sound of a business switching from one that had dictated for decades, to one humbly trying to understand what the customer wants.

It was the click of an industry that had, in effect, had to change from *transmit* to *receive* mode.

I've worked in the fashion business for more than twenty-five years. Looking back at the journey, I realise just how varied and rich it's been. This breadth of experience means I have a wide and unique understanding of wholesale, retail and ecommerce, what works and what doesn't. I've been directly responsible for huge collections at international level. Yet in stark contrast, only a few years later, I found myself sewing labels into my own collection in overheated offices in Ladbroke grove.

So – how on earth did this Chinese-Scottish woman of South African descent come to be in the fashion business in the first place? Why am I writing this book?

I was born in the north of Scotland as one of four children to academic parents. As far back as I can remember, I was always drawing. My mother, who was very creative, saw a spark in me and taught me to sew at a young age.

Once I'd mastered that skill, I realised how amazing it was to make a two-dimensional drawing into something you could actually wear. Then there was no holding me back. When I realised that there might be a possibility that I could make clothes and sell them, my interest in the fashion business was born.

By the age of thirteen, I was making clothes for myself, experimenting with fabrics, dyeing them, cutting and designing. My siblings were cajoled into being in my fashion shoots in our back garden. My parents, seeing that I was really driven, allowed me to use all my savings to create a small collection. By fifteen, I had succeeded in getting two stores in my local town to take a few pieces.

Although that was exciting for any teen, the pivotal moment came when at seventeen, I created an outfit which was selected to be shown on a catwalk at a local event. Fashion had found me.

It was no surprise to my parents that I wanted to pursue a career in fashion, and luckily they were both incredibly supportive. They encouraged me all the way, agreeing to let me leave school a year early to prepare a portfolio to apply for art college. I gained entry to Edinburgh College of Art, which was the only college offering a degree in fashion in the whole of Scotland.

In the second year, our head of department organised a field trip to Paris. When we got there, she revealed that we were going to the Chanel Couture Show at the iconic Rue Cambon headquarters. That one show triggered a lifelong passion for the business and had me truly hooked.

Passion for couture

The couture show in Paris set my mind whirling and I became curious to find out more about how couture was made. Understanding that I would never gain that knowledge in Scotland, I decided to get a job in London. I was thrilled when Victor Edelstein, the then London-based couturier (famous for dressing Diana), hired me.

Victor was on a mission to make his work on a par with the quality of Paris couture. We frequently dissected garments from Valentino and Dior in the studio – taking them apart piece by piece to analyse them. It was here that I learned the craft of creating fashion in its highest form.

After that, with even more passion and drive, I applied to the Royal College of Art, was accepted and completed my MA. With such great credentials, I left the UK to work in Italy and did not return for twelve years. Only now do I realise what a huge privilege it was, working closely with fashion legends in Milan. Those were the last years of a golden era before the internet; before digital; before the speed of the business shattered it.

Throughout my career I have been keenly interested in the fashion business, asking questions and grilling commercial directors for feedback. I was keen to understand whether designs or collections sold. The reason I'm writing this book is that I believe that having both design vision and an entrepreneurial approach to business is the key to a successful fashion brand today.

Changing landscape

Although I'm inclined to feel rather nostalgic about my early years in Milan, as an entrepreneur I'm already looking ahead. Fashion must move with the times, and now is the moment to recognise the huge shifts that digital has brought.

As a new era for the fashion business dawns, with it comes a brand new set of opportunities and rules. It's come so swiftly that it's left many businesses in total disarray, confused and bewildered about how to manage the changes. The period of steady predictable growth has come to an end. Finally, after years of the over-production of fashion collections flooding the shops and our wardrobes, the market's become saturated (not to mention uncertain). This has forced the business to rethink, and that makes me extremely happy. All of a sudden, the business is having to *reflect* on its intention, its integrity, the quality and value of the products and the transparency of where and how they are made. Digital has brought accountability, and for all of us that can only be a good thing.

'The digital revolution is like the steam age or an industrial revolution. We can't underestimate their depth and the fundamental nature of these changes.'
Paula Reed, Fashion and Brand Consultant

This is no doubt an exciting time for new brands, as social media and ecommerce have seemingly created a level playing field. A field where all creatives are able to carve out their own space.

However, the new democratised market place brings a new problem. It's so 'noisy' with products and images all competing for attention and customers that it's increasingly hard to be visible and stand out. The digital revolution has changed everything about how we experience the fashion business, from how we view it right through to how we buy it.

'For creative leaders and business executives, this has arguably been the most uncertain operating environment in living memory.' [1]
The Business of Fashion (BoF)/McKinsey,
The State of Fashion Report 2017

What's really changed? How can you adapt? Are you as a business ready to make the switch?

CHAPTER 1
Ten Influencing Factors

These ten influencing factors have changed the business for ever.

1. Receive mode

Digital has forced the industry to switch from transmit to receive mode – to becoming a listening/customer-facing business as customers take the driving seat.

However, many fashion houses were slow to react, banking on the strength of their brand name, and had to resort to spending more on lavish advertising and celebrities. When this strategy failed to produce the desired effect, they quickly developed ecommerce platforms and hired young teams to head up the social media and marketing, but it was rushed. Discerning consumers, meanwhile, were moving even faster in their demand for better online experience and service.

It's become clear that fashion businesses are no longer dictating. Instead, they're playing catch up with customers' needs. Those brands which have already built intellectual property (IP) are now working hard to keep their credibility, while every other fashion business is asking questions. In this challenging time for fashion, even the big brands have entered a period of self-reflection. They are consolidating their offer, cutting back the collections, dumping diffusion lines to refocus on what they stand for.

'*The big trend now is everyone pulling back, really identifying who they are, identifying who their customer is, servicing their customer, and really showing their strengths in their products. If it's someone that is famous for prints, they're really emphasising the prints; if it's someone that is very strong on shoes and handbags, they're really emphasising that. I don't think a customer wants everything from everyone, they want to go to the expert in each product category.*'
Graeme Black, Creative Director and Owner, Graeme Black

2. Connected and engaged

The industry has had to switch from delayed feedback to reaching out and communicating with customers directly and in real time.

'*In 2016, of a population of 7.4 billion, 3.5 billion were connected.*

In 2021, it's predicted that of a population of 8 billion, 7 billion will be connected.' [1]
From *Ericsson Mobility Report* 2017

We are living in an extraordinary new age of connectivity. With almost 7 billion people predicted to be online by 2021, that's a lot of individual voices, opinions and expectations to meet.

This means everyone on the planet (give or take a few) will have more access to the internet, which in turn produces more data. For any businesses creating *product*, this forces an abandonment of a scatter gun approach. Instead, businesses need a strategic revision of how best to serve and then engage to retain customers, wherever they may be.

3. I want it yesterday

Customers are pushing to take delivery of purchases in shorter and shorter timeframes. Manufacturers in the last few years have grown accustomed to requests for a faster and 'closer to the season' supply. Even the more luxury manufacturers are revising their methods to accommodate change, increase flexibility and streamline processes. This is because the market is so unpredictable and businesses want to avoid stock commitment if they can.

Suppliers have been watching the market moves with close interest. If the fashion show schedules move, then their production schedules move too. This causes massive disruption to logistics and huge headaches for the manufacturers.

Other businesses are seizing the opportunity to sidestep these issues, looking at product chain disruption. Take for example the UK brand Unmade. They have blended technology and fashion together delivering a fully fashioned customised jacquard sweater to customers in eight weeks rather a than a traditional timeline of eight months. This hugely alters their cash flow and business model.

4. All change

We are living in a world that accommodates not only a new era of technology, but four different generations with different values, desires and buying habits. Mobile-savvy Baby Boomers seek value for money, Generation X are still quite independent in their reasons to buy, while Generation Y rely on the opinion of others. They prefer to rent than own and spend more on experiences, while Generation Z conversely want to own everything and are hugely influenced by social media.

5. Volatility

There are numerous factors that are influencing people's buying behaviours. Let's take a few as an example:

- Political unrest causing currency fluctuations
- Trade agreements changing
- Terrorism causing changes in travel habits and security
- Showing or not showing and wearing status symbols (China)
- Generations looking for transparency
- Experience of shopping in-store or online
- Spending on experience and food rather than clothes
- Delivery by drone or 3D printing at home
- Augmented and virtual reality in retail
- Introduction of artificial intelligence

These unpredictable factors can happen overnight and have caught big corporates by surprise. Through digital we can become aware of these changes in real time, so our behaviour changes in real time. This ties in of course with the nature of fashion, which is fluid.

6. Experience

It's official: people are now using mobile devices more than laptops. We use them while we are shopping, checking prices and reviews. This blending and blurring of technology and reality makes it apparent that the role of retail is set to change rapidly. The traditional consumer has gone, and so will the old retailers. As it becomes more likely that a brand will be experienced first through technology than real life, the role of bricks and mortar fashion retail will pivot. To keep customers in-store and make them more likely to purchase there, retailers need to break down the barrier between shopper and product.

Shops are set to become an experience of the brand – showrooms and spaces in which to weave dreams. Big brands have realised that consumers crave unique and curated in-store experiences that are backed up with a mirrored experience online.

Once shops have become more of a 'showroom' experience and the scene is set for customers to become the focus, they will then be likely to make their purchase online.

'Physical retail is really important. We live in a world where we have to use technology, and a lot of successful shops use multi-channel. They either have a parallel website or social media, but customers still want to go to the store and have that amazing experience. They want smell, speech – the whole emotive experience, which they don't get online.'

Maria Lemos, Founder and Director of Rainbowwave

7. Global/local

With so much of the planet now interconnected, it's become apparent that the tools we were using to communicate and engage with customers were blunt and unrepresentative. Through data, we can now observe in more granular detail than ever the needs, wishes and desires of each demographic. Global brands are investing in understanding local customers, nurturing them and providing a more localised and curated offer.

8. Transparency

Consumers have become super-savvy, using enhanced technology to check pricing and compare reviews before buying. Brands that once had prices that were hidden or fluctuated across different platforms/currencies/points of sale have been obliged to clean up their act in a bid to show transparency and gain back customer trust.

> ' *I think the fashion industry has had a lot of bad press. Revelations such as child labour, bad working conditions, exploitations, etc., are creating distrust. People are asking, "Am I sure where my T-shirt has come from? Has someone suffered for creating this?" I can tell you this as I work with students and they really do care.* '
>
> Grit Seymour, Creative Director

Brands themselves are now open to more scrutiny as consumers are seeking reassurances that the *product is genuine and the price relates to the value they feel they are getting.* Similarly, sourcing and sustainability have become increasingly important to customers.

9. Show time

It was the spectacle of the Chanel Couture Show that had me completely hooked on fashion. That's because it was an experience – a live performance, entertainment.

As more and more brands saturated the catwalk schedule, and buyers and press alike reached overload, the industry began to realise this format was becoming outdated. The question arose – what's the point? Images are streamed live and the catwalk experience is therefore no longer aimed at buyers and the press, but is more for general consumption, so the return on investment is no longer clear.

It soon dawned on designers that the attendees were more interested in being seen at the show than looking at the collection. Secondly, their hard work was being published online and copied so quickly that it was becoming brand-damaging.

In a bid to keep on top of the changes, brands have abandoned the one-rule-fits-all schedule. While it's a relief to see change, it's left an uncertain landscape for shows and presentations as everyone experiments on how and when to showcase. The show schedule conundrum rolls on, with luxury brands debating a straight-to-consumer model of buying from catwalk, while smaller brands without the financial backing are left pondering their next steps.

' *Whether it is possible to maintain margins while keeping fashion's fussiest consumers excited and engaged by investing heavily in the manipulation of an increasingly complex fashion cycle remains to be seen.*' [2]
BoF/McKinsey, *The State of Fashion Report 2017*

With our voracious appetite for fashion images, shows have become spectacles for everyone to enjoy, consume and share – more an experience and entertainment than an industry-specific show. Luxury brands have made a quick move to pour more cash into their shows, making them extreme and excessive in a bid to keep their image above and beyond what others might achieve. Chanel and LVMH are the leaders in this, regularly spending £2m on one show.

10. The new guard

When I began in the industry, we were very much working from and influenced by print magazines. The fashion shows were exclusive events for buyers from wholesale stores and the press.

The front row has completely swapped around – bloggers and celebrities have now taken prime seats, as they are the personalities with the biggest social media presence. Even model castings are biased towards people with a substantial social media following. Traditional PR strategy has had to be completely rethought. There was a certain order and hierarchy which has completely changed – all as a result of technology.

So let's just say the rulebook has been torn up. Yes, digital has changed fashion for ever. Therein lies the opportunity. Now is the time to take advantage...

‘ ... to challenge everything that has gone before them. The rulebook has been torn and the opportunity is there for some-body to rip it to bits. They just have to have the guts to do it, because the world is crying out for something new.’

Mathew Dixon, Global Managing Director, Karen Harvey Consulting Group

How to adapt

Owners are often so busy running the business that they fail to work on building the business. In this new fast-paced environment, those who don't wake up to the switch will disappear fast.

'Ever since the 70s, the fashion system hasn't really changed. With digital everything has changed. Many of the old companies, which are not fast enough, just tend to disappear, which we've seen happen already. It's the ones that are too rigid and inflexible that won't make it.'

Grit Seymour, Creative Director

So now we understand what's switched, how are we in the business able to adapt? If we are to re-evaluate and consolidate our businesses, make our offers sharper, clearer and more concise, where do we start?

When a creative director is hired by a brand, the first thing they do is immerse themselves in the brand's archives. If you go through the press releases of every new high-profile appointment, they always refer to the archives, using words such as 'history of the brand', 'the brand's DNA' and 'heritage'.

This is what I did on the day I started as design director of Missoni M. My remit was to create a diffusion line for Missoni for a big company called Marzotto, which had agreed a licencing deal with the family. Anyone who joins the company first has a full immersion day in the archives and then visits the family home on the lakes north of Milan to meet everyone at head office. It came as a bit of a shock to me as only the day before I had been finalising the presentation for my last season at Armani. From one day to the next, I was catapulted from a world of beige and tonal colours to another bursting with joyful colour, texture and pattern – two family businesses with two very different points of view. The experience left me with a clear message of what the Missoni brand stood for. Its fashion comes from an authentic point of view. No great surprise, then, that its brands have survived generations.

It was through working closely with these fashion icons that I realised the key to their long-term brand success is that they are the living, breathing example of their brand. Their personal brand is perfectly aligned with their brand culture.

Why then, during my years of working with other fashion businesses, have I found that the brand DNA just does not exist? I have found their brand messages as muddled and unclear as their customer targets. I realised that although these businesses may have started their brand journey with a plan and mission statement, and even found a product niche, they failed to create a master plan for the long term. They've certainly not reacted quickly enough to changing fashion tastes.

So how does brand success work for a smaller company?

Back in 2011 I met with Clare Hornby and her partner Emma Howarth. They had co-founded and run ecommerce fashion company ME+EM for a few years. They had a growing database and business. Things where looking positive, until they hit a glitch. They called me as their previous designer had left them high and dry half way through the season. There was no collection and they were now months behind schedule. How to get a collection designed in only four weeks?

I did in fact manage to help them that season and created a great collection in only a few weeks. They were so relieved, and I could tell they were keen to learn, so I explained what they could do to improve their process and business.

Over the next few years, working closely with Clare and Emma on their business, I helped develop their creative vision and align it to their brand message. I created a clear design DNA, showed them how a design-led business worked and how to create the exceptional product that they had hoped for. The results were astounding with their turnover quadrupling over the three years we worked together.

A few years in, one of the partners left and the remaining partner became the creative lead. She seized the opportunity to become the face behind the brand and set about creating brand personality and culture. Today she is the brand's living, breathing personality, wearing the clothes, opening up her life and the process behind the label, and connecting with customers. Coming from a high-level marketing background, she was clever enough to make that move and it's worked. Now a firmly established brand, they have won many industry accolades and successfully found investors for their next stage of growth.

Many companies are pivoting and diverting their funds into digital marketing and ecommerce. However, if they miss out the crucial step of working out who they are and what they stand for before they launch, their brand journey will be short-lived.

Why are foundations so important?

There is one fundamental reason and that's because everything has become personal. Businesses need to create something authentic and continually have to revise and strengthen their mission statement and purpose. If the purpose comes from the top, then all the better.

'The creative industry has totally changed. Everyone from CEOs to all the people behind the scenes are becoming brands. This is the age of personal branding.'

Caroline Issa, Fashion Director and CEO of Tank

Once you create your foundation, you are in a better postilion to clarify your uniqueness and originality. This in turn gives you the confidence to stake your claim to your space in the market and attract opportunities to grow your brand.

The fashion businesses is in a period of painfully learning to adapt. The challenges facing owner-led independent businesses are unique. They are caught between the luxury of known brands with unlimited budgets to pour into powerful branding and marketing strategies, and young up-and-coming brands which are more digitally savvy and agile. From experience, I've found they frequently lack the level of expertise and insights into their team and business to take both their product and brand to the next level.

So now, in addition to being overworked, stressed about cash flow and production, independent business owners have a new key challenge:

How to remain credible, visible and grow in such a competitive market.

So who is helping these businesses? In short, there are plenty of books out on the market that can tell you how to *set up* a fashion business. Others can tell you how to *survive* in the business. There are articles upon articles about the woes of the business, yet no one is offering a *solution*.

So, I want to help, and these are the reasons why:

Because now is the time for smaller creative businesses. Although they might not have the mighty financial power of the big corporate companies, smaller companies do have the ability to turn an agile and forward-thinking fashion business into a successful, sustainable fashion brand of the future.

Because a change of mindset is the key. I realised the key to success when working with my clients. Indeed, I proved that I was using a process that worked. If I could help other brands understand the process, lend them my insights, then they would avoid years of wondering how to get ahead.

Because I'm fed up of mediocrity. It makes me mad to see people waste time and money on marketing when the brand and product are not right. I've witnessed it first-hand. I want to see fashion businesses wake up, be more professional, be accountable and less wasteful.

Because I've been there, done that. This last reason is the one I feel most passionately about. I don't want independent owners to lose the business they have worked so hard to create just because they lack access to expertise/knowledge. I've been there and know it's painful.

The solution

This book aims to provide the solution by taking a hard look at what's happening and to acknowledge fully that we are in a time of consolidation. It aims to clarify what's at the heart of a brand that succeeds despite the many challenges of the market and explain it in a clear and helpful way. However, if we do this without understanding future opportunities then we will miss the point of *clever consolidation*.

'*There's a big gap between the traditional businesses and new ones popping up with completely different rules, strategies, timings. They are redefining the business and rewriting the rules that have been there for centuries.*'

Grit Seymour, Creative Director

In this most challenging of times for the fashion business, as we move into uncharted territory, the old rules no longer can be applied. So what replaces them?

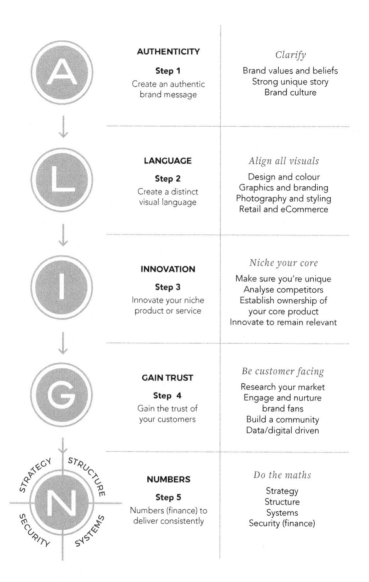

AUTHENTICITY

Step 1

Create an authentic
brand message

Clarify

Brand values and beliefs
Strong unique story
Brand culture

LANGUAGE

Step 2

Create a distinct
visual language

Align all visuals

Design and colour
Graphics and branding
Photography and styling
Retail and eCommerce

INNOVATION

Step 3

Innovate your niche
product or service

Niche your core

Make sure you're unique
Analyse competitors
Establish ownership of
your core product
Innovate to remain relevant

GAIN TRUST

Step 4

Gain the trust of
your customers

Be customer facing

Research your market
Engage and nurture
brand fans
Build a community
Data/digital driven

NUMBERS

Step 5

Numbers (finance) to
deliver consistently

Do the maths

Strategy
Structure
Systems
Security (finance)

15

CHAPTER 2

The Five Steps of Alignment

When you first fall in love with fashion, that bug gets under your skin and becomes part of you for life. It has to be the most dynamic, fun and creative business, ever-changing, and it is never dull.

However, I've discovered you need more than passion. Over my twenty-five years of experience working with companies, I've realised that it's the alignment of creative and business vision from the outset that determines their success.

Despite these challenging times for the fashion business, opportunities await those who are brave, focused and aim high. I believe that the secret to achieving visibility and growth in today's market, to make that *switch from a business that struggles to one that grows steadily and takes full advantage of the opportunities digital presents*, requires alignment of five key areas inside the business.

The ALIGN Principle

- (A) **authentic** brand message
- (L) visual **language**
- (I) innovate and create IP
- (G) **gain** customer trust
- (N) **numbers** (finance) to deliver consistency

For a fashion business to stand out and grow, it must ensure it expresses an *authentic brand message* in a consistent, recognisable and creative *language*. It has to offer something unique in the market *(innovation and IP)* and must be customer facing in order to *gain* the customers' trust. Trust is built by great communication and delivering consistently. Consistent delivery in terms of product and customer experience requires funding and systems, so financial planning is essential.

Step 1 – Authentic brand message.

'Since 2008 the number of articles that mention the word authenticity in the headline has risen dramatically overall.'[1]
Harvard Review 2016

To be heard and seen in today's competitive market, you need to have a succinct and authentic brand message which customers can connect with, interpreted through original creative vision and backed up, of course, with unique product.

So why in the digital age is the word 'authentic' becoming so important?

Where fashion business is concerned it's because clients are looking for a clear brand message that resonates with them. As with politics, every aspect of fashion has been questioned. There is a general sense of disillusionment and distrust, and customers today are looking for transparency and honesty. They are inundated with so many products while the time for decision making continues to decrease, so clarity of message is paramount. You must have a purpose and key principles in order to build the story of that message. If you look at the fashion businesses that are thriving, they're the ones with authenticity shining through.

Step 2 – Visual language. Taking the time to create distinct visual references and touch points that match and deliver according to the principles and purpose of your business is a massively rewarding process. This means pulling together references and creating a set of 'brand boards' – everything visual that you would like to show up when someone searches for your brand name. Create a visual language that customers will recognise.

It's such a wonderful process, but it's often passed over because the business:

- didn't have the time
- didn't have the budget or expertise
- had no idea why it was important

If you take a few creative days out of your schedule, turn off your phone and switch off your computer, then you can transform the way you think about your business. Creating brand boards, even if they are not beautifully executed, promotes a sense of clarity and confidence. Then you can brief designers and suppliers and your staff better, articulate your message to potential future partners, and use it in your business plans.

At Ted Baker, everyone knows what's Ted and what's not. Whether they're choosing which manufacturer to place an order with or selecting a print, they are clear what represents the brand and what doesn't. Make it your business to create that clarity and brand culture for you and your team.

Step 3 – Innovate. Once you have your authenticity and visual language clear, the next step is to innovate within your market sector and create assets in your business.

To strengthen your business, work out clearly what single aspect of it is unique to you – your USP – and own it. It might be a core product or the way you deliver it, or perhaps it's an original way in which you engage the customer.

Being able to innovate in your niche means you need to understand the market, constantly researching and challenging the space that you are working in. Successful businesses are always on the lookout for new angles and opportunities. Typically, on one day of the week, big businesses will have team meetings to talk about what has worked and what has not, and lessons learned. It's a great discipline to nurture – it's the difference between thinking you are different and knowing you are.

Use your authentic brand message and visual language and push your team to create ideas and intellectual property. Be curious about how technology is affecting manufacture. Push the boundaries, and you will find even with such a crowded market that you can create something new. You may feel at times that you are throwing the baby out with the bathwater, but be bold and confident when you lock on to what you really want to be known for.

It's common for brands to become unstuck. From season to season, as they try to build up a customer base and show something exciting to the press, their clarity gets lost. They may have had a clear offer at the start, but wholesalers and stores need constant freshness. Sadly, if businesses are chasing the figures and looking to please, their once-strong brand can become confused, diluted, and worst of all, inconsistent. Inconsistency spells disaster for any brand as clients get confused and eventually lose interest.

Step 4 – Gain trust. In the past, it was possible to begin with an idea or point of view. Now you have to find a niche in the market and create a solution for your customer. Aligning what you stand for with an exceptional product (or service or experience) that the customer wants is the key to your brand's growth.

This is a unique period where we have customers from four generations with four sets of beliefs, wants and needs.

Growing your business means getting out there and engaging in their space so they can tell you how to improve. Ask questions and do surveys. Home in on your target customer and understand everything about them. Once you get them on board and they become loyal, make sure they are motivated to spread the news.

Remember – don't try to be everything to everyone. It just doesn't work anymore.

Step 5 – Numbers. My fellow RCA graduate designer Neil Barrett recently said in his interview in the BoF that the secret behind the growth of his €90million business was delivering rigorously and consistently. *However, this* is the biggest challenge for business owners and unfortunately takes up most of their working day.

> ' *Consistent delivery and great product follow consistent delivery of production. This only follows if you are organized with the whole process and have a critical path that you stick to.*'
> Kate Hills, Founder of Make It British

A lot of this angst, I have noticed, is down to inefficiency and lack of process, systems and expertise. Some owners forget about the numbers and hope that LVMH or the Kering Group will come calling and buy their brand. While a miracle might happen, they won't see it if their heads are in the sand.

Aligning your goals with a route to finance to support the delivery of great product is what allows the business to grow.

There are so many pay-offs when you align this final part of the puzzle. Structuring the team to work more efficiently, putting in systems and processes that save both time and money, is hard work, but I guarantee that the effort really does pay off. However, once you have worked out what you are delivering to whom and when, then diligently worked through the other four parts of ALIGN, you need to make an appointment with your finance team or accountant to see how the numbers are stacking up. Many owners are afraid to do this, partly because they might not like the result of a number crunch, and others just prefer to roll along, living hand to mouth. This is not a great way to work, though, as avoiding numbers can lead to business decline and closure, despite you working every hour God sends.

Having all five parts of the business aligned, you and your team can concentrate on innovating and pushing for better fabrics, fit, product and photography. Trust me, your team will be happier, work more effectively, be more motivated and feel part of the plan as a result.

The order is important

I have worked hard to put these alignment steps in the right order so it's no use skipping any out or moving them around. If you do the finance before you know what your focus product is going to be, you will likely have to do the calculations all over again. If you create a new range before you work out what its purpose is, then the result will be off target. Doing this process methodically will mean you are totally clear on your next steps, and you are equipped and ready to take your business up a level.

When you and your team are ready and able to describe

your brand succinctly, why it's unique, and details of your business workings at a moment's notice, the results are likely to astound you. I've seen the transformation with the companies I've worked with, and the confidence they have after learning the know-how of international brands. People sit up and take them seriously. Better suppliers consider working with them as they have the critical path all worked out. They know the price points they want to achieve and can give realistic indications of quantity and delivery. Better photographers and agents work with them because they stick to their schedule. Buyers know where to find them, what they stand for and where to place their products in stores. Everyone they do business with can describe their brand and pass on the authentic brand message behind their label.

If you can excite your *buyers* then they can excite their customers. In time you will find your true and loyal customer base. If you lose some because of your newfound focus, because you are niching and delivering something exceptional, then you will gain many more than you lose.

Not only is the ALIGN method a clear and simple way to view your own company and analyse your business strengths and weaknesses, it's also a powerful tool that enables you to benchmark your business against your competitors. This in turn enables you to work out what makes a business fail or succeed today.

'*No brand is immune to the changes that are happening in the market. Indeed, big household names too are falling by the wayside. Fashion retailers are still following the same patterns of overbuying and deep discounting and consumers are reluctant to pay full price. Retailers have responded by spending less on their lines, when what they need to be doing instead is addressing these problems more proactively. Rather than chasing after the same "micro trends" as their competitors they need to work on what their customer wants and to fulfil their needs.'*[2]

Glen Tooke, Consumer Insight Director, Kantar Worldpanel

The ALIGN *method delivers a new approach and a change of mentality.* I've observed seven common mistakes in businesses that really need alignment. See if any of this sounds familiar:

1. They have no business pitch. The owner can't say with confidence or authority what they do, what they stand for, or what part of the market they own.

2. They lack strong creative and strategic vision. They are just following the same path as others, hoping it will succeed. They don't have a higher purpose or clear strategy for the long term.

3. They lack creative expertise. Without highly trained experts, creative clarity and brand vision, a brand's foundations are weak. Having these in place (or not) from the outset makes (or breaks) a company.

4. They are badly organised. Sloppy and unprofessional businesses are missing huge opportunities as they are too busy sorting stuff out.

5. They lack direction from the top. The business owner is unclear what the brand stands for. If they can't communicate this internally, then the team will not be able to deliver. Everyone they hire into their company is likely to want to put their spin on things, so a business owner needs to be very clear.

6. Reluctance to do the maths. I'm adamant that business owners should be realistic about what they are trying to achieve in their business. To make it a success, they have to focus on whether the finance of the business works and is sustainable not just season to season, but for the longer term.

7. The owner only works on the bits they like. This is fine if they're not expecting much from their business. The thing is, if they want more, all five parts of ALIGN need to be given careful attention.

The *good news* is that the ALIGN process is on-going and creative, so you can revisit and revise it many times. With a new mindset and approach, you can enjoy the whole journey.

Benchmarking brands with ALIGN

Austin Reed closed its doors in 2016. I use the framework of ALIGN to identify what might have gone wrong. How did they score?

(A) **yes.** It had 125 years of authentic brand history.

(L) **no.** The creative language was weak.

(I) **no.** It failed to innovate.

(G) **yes,** but it banked on the trust gained from an old customer base.

(N) **no.** The numbers and finance were too exposed in the retail sector and the company failed to develop its digital presence.

In my opinion, a failure to move with the times meant Austin Reed lost its market share. Combined with exposure to retail space and rising overheads, it went through years of losses before eventually closing.

Jaeger, another iconic British brand, has also gone into

administration. Again, using the steps can we identify what went wrong?

- (A) **yes.** It had 125 years of authentic brand history.
- (L) **no.** The creative language was erratic.
- (I) **no.** No innovation nor niche product was identified.
- (G) **no.** The company lost sight of what it solved for customers.
- (N) **no.** The numbers and finance were too exposed in the retail sector and the company failed to develop its digital presence.

I've identified that Jaeger lost sight of its identity, but more crucially forgot what solution its brand served in the customer's wardrobe. Its erratic creative added even more confusion.

How sad to see these great British heritage brands disappear. What missed opportunities! Their stories serve as clear examples that today, no one can afford to have some parts of their business working and others not.

Now let's look at a UK success story, Orlebar Brown. Adam Brown and partners have, in seven short years, grown a niche brand from £0 to £10 million. How do they score and what are they doing right?

- (A) **yes.** Adam and his partners created an authenticity around one product, swimming shorts.
- (L) **yes.** The creative language is clear and consistent.
- (I) **yes.** They are always looking to deliver innovation.
- (G) **yes.** They deliver great swimwear with guarantees and no quibble returns.
- (N) **yes.** The business has grown though meticulous planning and complete understanding of the numbers and finance.

Adam has cornered the market in one strong niche and his brand serves a real purpose. This combined with great digital engagement and innovation means that he has an organically growing business with die-hard brand fans.

Let me show you another example going deeper into the method. I was recently contacted by a well-known UK-based yoga brand that was struggling despite its strong customer base. I assessed the business against the ALIGN principle.

Ⓐ **yes.** The business had a great brand message and had managed to create authenticity with eco-friendly fabrics, sustainable production and comfort. The owner lived her principles, looking healthily glowing, and was a great role model for her brand.

Ⓛ **no.** There was a distinct lack of creative direction, so in five years of business the company had slipped behind other competitor brands. In an attempt to boost sales, it opened up the collection, which made the development time consuming and costly. The collection became too large and unfocused, with much replication. The company had missed the whole 'athleisure' trend, and its photography was staid and traditional.

Ⓘ **no.** There was little innovation either in fabrics or design. Lack of knowledge and expertise led the brand to become staid, and therefore sales began to decrease. The company was looking for progress and newness, but had not challenged its suppliers to help with pushing the product forward.

Ⓖ **yes.** The brand engaged well with consumers on ecommerce, building up a real community, and had a great social media following. Customers frequently came back to buy as the product was well made, but moved away as it lacked newness.

Ⓝ **no.** The numbers did not work. Predominantly the cost of developing an overly large collection with a lack of brand identity meant overheads got higher as the sales began to slide. This combination sadly meant closure.

A key issue for the owner was that adhering to her principles, such as eco-friendly fabrics and working with manufactures that showed sustainable and transparent production, meant the price of the collection was higher than her competitors. If there is a good reason behind a higher price, it needs to be part of the USP and built into the business strategy. Being able to demonstrate value and articulate clearly why customers should pay a price over and above the competition is vital to a brand's success. In this particular case, I showed the client what her brand might look like under my direction, how to create a visual language to match her brand values and how to work harder to innovate in the market. She was impressed by the change of approach, and sorry that she had not worked on it earlier.

Where are you in your journey?

You have the ability to make a difference to your business. All your hard work and creative output will come to nothing if you lose your market share to a competitor who is more forward thinking. I've seen it happen.

This is a great time to take advantage as everyone is playing catch-up. If you put the time in to fine tune and align your business now, it might mean you stay another season in business, and that *one season* could be the one that sees your breakthrough.

Hate to say this, but it's true: 'If you snooze, you lose.'

CHAPTER 3
Authenticity

Here's James. (James isn't real, but don't tell him that.) James's company sells contemporary men's T-shirts using Japanese fabrics which have a great fit. They are priced at £85, which is in line with his competitors, but he is a young business so feedback says his price seems quite high. He knows his T-shirts are great and his current customers do too, but he's struggling to get that message across.

Should he drop the price?

One of the biggest challenges the fashion business faces is how to articulate the value of its products. In the past, before ecommerce, you might have asked a sales assistant for prices when you visited a store. Digital allows customers real-time access to research price and value in a way they previously never could.

'*Part of the reason why consumers have been able to seek discounts and promotions has been their uptake of ecommerce and digital tools, which has created price transparency across brands and regions.*'[1]

BoF/McKinsey, *The State of Fashion Report 2017*

Prices used to fluctuate depending on where you shopped, and were mostly hidden or not even displayed. Often customers felt hoodwinked if they found the same item in another store at a lesser price, but many of the price differences were linked to international price discrepancies, or in some cases a lack of company strategy, especially for designer brands, to set the wholesale recommended retail price (RRP) consistently across all points of sale. The currency changes are still an issue, but many brands have dealt with this issue via ecommerce platforms and can now show and sell in multiple currencies.

So with digital, consumers are far more informed, savvy, and likely to make sure that they are paying the best price for any given item. Then they evaluate whether the product is worth the price tag. Brands that realised their reputation was at risk addressed, as far as possible, the discrepancies across their pricing to make sure wherever the customer shops, the price is the same. Today garments are priced clearly making choice much easier. Everything has become more transparent.

So, can James get away with a higher price if his customers know that his product is worth it?

Yes, he can. But he needs to tell his customers about the T-shirt. It will remain an ordinary mass-produced T-shirt until customers know there's a story behind it. Care and attention went into its perfection. James's product is genuine and authentic. Your product needs to be too.

We'll come back to James later, but for now, it's your challenge to find and develop your very own:

Authentic Brand Message

We know that customers want transparency and honesty, and they want to know a product is genuine and authentic. Today they are looking for the 'soul' behind the brand. A lot of established brands already have soul.

'I think the equation came naturally to the first designers, such Armani or Dolce Gabbana, who all have very strong roots, heritage and heavy influences. They express themselves rather than design. Today, style has to be rooted in values, beliefs and something deeper.'

Andrea Ciccoli, Co-founder of The Level Group

Development of an authentic message, a system of beliefs and higher values, in today's market is critical. If you have no story behind the product, you can't engage emotionally. It doesn't matter how amazing your collection is, if there is no inbuilt integrity of intention, then any initial brand success will probably be short-lived.

So now we have talked about the *message*, but even more important is the move to show complete transparency behind the manufacturing process. The disastrous collapse of the Rana Plaza building in Bangladesh in 2013 showed the public the tragic cost of cheap manufacture. And we can be pretty certain that something like this will happen again. There will always be a voracious hunger for cheap fashion, so it will be a long time before we can eradicate the use of cheap labour.

But for the wider fashion industry, especially the mid to

luxury sector, it's left an indelible mark. Suddenly everyone has realised what a wasteful and exploitative industry fashion can be. This fuelled a general distrust, especially among the younger shoppers who are keen to understand where a product comes from.

In a bid to counteract this distrust, the forward-thinking brands, from luxury to high street, are now opening their businesses and showing their authenticity through the process of creating their products. They are looking to change the way they are perceived, seeking incentives to show they care for the process and environment.

'This is an area that offers real benefits for fashion brands, whether mass-market or luxury, as all companies are under pressure to increase transparency on inputs and reveal more of the pedigree of their products.'[2]

BoF/McKinsey, The State of Fashion Report 2017

Take, for example, the hugely successful high street retailer, H&M. Since 2013, H&M has offered a worldwide garment collection initiative, and to date has collected 40,000 tonnes of textiles and clothes which will be recycled instead of going to landfill. The company is now pushing to create new fibres and garments from the waste. Although the technology to do this has existed for years, this is an ambitious project on a large scale.

'Recent events have found the fashion industry, like many others, more fearful and cautious, especially in Paris, the crucible of the luxury business…A senior representative of LVMH said *their executives were re-examining their plans for 2016 in the light of what's now appropriate. Appropriate behaviour has become an industry obsession. So has authenticity.*[3]

Jo Ellison, Fashion Journalist, *Financial Times*

An example of this shift in the market to show the inner working of the process and engage with the customer is Karl Lagerfeld's recent Chanel couture show. He moved the whole couture staff from the atelier on Rue Cambon, along with all their equipment, including cutting tables, dummies, sewing machines, fabrics, embroidery materials and canvas toiles, and used this as the backdrop for the show. During the show, the staff continued to work as if back at HQ.

Mr Lagerfeld is a clever man and reacts to the zeitgeist. If transparency is needed, if complete honesty is required, then how better to convince your client than have the merit and value of the price tag displayed in all its bare reality?

'Behind the girls in the show, there are 200 more who make what they wear – that's quite a lot, no? And I thought we should show them to the public too.' [4]

Karl Lagerfeld, speaking to style.com

'...a demonstration, proof, really, of the actual value of haute couture, it couldn't have been clearer or more awe-inspiring.' [5]

Sarah Mower, Fashion Critic reviewing Lagerfeld's show

Likewise, sustainability has now become a focus of the industry. For fifteen years it has been the integrity behind the designer brand Stella McCartney.

'*Sustainability is becoming an important new driver of consumers' purchasing decisions. In emerging markets, for example, more than 65 percent of consumers actively seek out sustainable fashion.*'[6]

BoF/McKinsey, *The State of Fashion Report 2017*

Despite the many doubters who said that sustainable and ethically minded businesses could never become a commercial reality, Stella McCartney has proved her case. With her collection distributed to over 100 countries and listing 600 wholesale accounts, her business has been a staggering British success story.

The customer can smell a fake

From the very beginning, Stella McCartney was vocal about her beliefs and values, eschewing real leather and fur for fake substitutes. She made it part of her brand mission and shaped her team and expertise around it. Her mission is personal, and that is reflected in her business. This is her authentic brand message. She is listed as one of the BoF's top 500 'People Shaping the Global Fashion Business'.

'*Sustainability is now enshrined in the company's values, embedded in its culture and reflected in the team of experts that McCartney has built. They shape the company's sustainability policies, its underlying business model and its brand message in line with her mission.*'[7]

BoF, Top Influencing 500

Another brand, the brainchild of one of the new generation of entrepreneurs who has a strong authentic brand message around sustainability, is UK-based Tom Cridland's collection, or rather project. His 30 Year items, such as the 30 Year Sweatshirt, have captured the attention of the public. 'Durable, luxury clothing at an affordable price point' has resonated across the globe. *Fortune* magazine wrote 'if more designers were like Cridland, one day "fast fashion" could be as "out" as last season's designs are today.'

This is a wonderful, simple message that we could 'buy less, buy better'. *It is a different sort of sustainability from Stella McCartney's luxury brand.*

The signs of change

The fashion business used to be a predicable machine, working to predictable schedules and selling to a predictable customer base that bought in a predictable pattern at predictable times of the year. All that has changed.

The manufacturers and brands that are flourishing today are those that have adopted a more global, digital and collaborative approach. They saw the need to specialise to accentuate their strengths, highlight their quality and update their systems.

In Milan, the first sign of the change was when the euro was introduced. With less disposable income, local customers began to avoid the luxury fashion stores and were replaced with an international clientele from China, Russia and the Middle East. Italian manufacturers and brands then knew it was time to begin collaborating and partnering with high-end brands in growth markets like China. No longer able to sit on the laurels of being the best producers of luxury goods, they had to become more proactive and open-minded. Luckily for the Italians, being masters of artisan craftsmanship, tradition and authenticity, they already had a rich foundation of storytelling to build on.

I've found that if a brand lacks a story and engaging narrative, then it gets stuck. It is unable to build loyalty, and so finds it hard to grow its business. Research is proving that consumers are motivated to buy because they *want* something rather than *need* it. Furthermore, women make a decision based on a *feeling* and men on *thinking*.

Whatever the truth is behind consumer behaviour, we know that people take action through emotion. That extra reason to buy comes from a compelling, authentic brand message. It's this that differentiates one product from another.

When I work with business owners, I like to look at their businesses from the start and dig deep into their motivations and aspirations. On examining their brands more closely and how they're developed, I've discovered many of them have wandered off track. Quite often it's due to production, and the limitations of what they can achieve with their 'tool-kit'. Sometimes it's a reflection of what the market's buying, which isn't what they want to create. Most often, however, it's because the cycle is so relentless that business owners don't have time to sit back and think with clarity.

'I think consistency is absolutely key, and to know who and what your brand is, to be able to answer any question on it inside out in terms of who your customer is, what your brand stands for, what your brand's message and aesthetic are. Keep moving it forward, but stay true to what your brand actually is. I think the worst thing that a brand can do is chop and change.'

Barry Woods, Managing Director, Life Fashion Recruitment

To lose your identity, to lack brand foundations in these turbulent times, spells trouble. Just observe the revolving door of creative directors in the luxury brands. The brands that have consistency are the ones which strengthen their position as global brands.

Take Hermes, for example. While the designers have changed, the aesthetic and brand are bigger than the designer at the helm. We have seen a shift from banking on the strength of one person's creative vision to partnerships and teams focusing on getting back to brand roots, connecting with customers and rebuilding trust and authenticity.

So, what's happened?

> ‘ I think there has been this almost gluttony of too many stores, people losing themselves, losing their DNA, losing the reason why a customer went to them. It's all become too generic, and I feel that the crisis has come about by this kind of desire to try and be everything to everyone, and I don't think that works.’
>
> Graeme Black, Creative Director and Owner, Graeme Black

Building brand culture

Successful owners have a way of being that permeates through the company and staff. It's because their purpose and brand message are clear.

I'm going to start with an example. Giorgio Armani's business is today worth $5.8 billion and he is listed as 196 in the Forbes List of Billionaires 2016.

CASE STUDY - ARMANI

Back in the mid-90s, I was approached by Giorgio Armani to work with his company as the design director of his lucrative Collezioni. I was very privileged indeed to come into his business at a point where it was still growing and he had just moved the whole business from its gorgeous home on Via Borgonuovo 21, to larger offices on the same street.

The new studio was a bright, long corridor of glass walls and doors with pale grey carpets and cream walls. The shuttered windows looked on to the courtyard. On each desk, there was an identical stationery kit – one picture frame, one pencil box, one tray for white paper, and some shelves. We were under strict instructions not to have anything personal out on display and to keep the space clear and tidy.

It dawned on me that this was the first time I'd worked as a designer for a truly international brand where the owner's vision was so strong it covered the smallest detail of his designers' offices and what he expected of them.

This might seem a little extreme, but a designer who has strong views on how the offices are set out and how the staff behave in that environment sets a strong culture.

Giorgio Armani is a living, breathing example of what gives a fashion business a simple, clear, authentic brand message.

Can you be like Armani? You are allowed to have more than one pencil box if you wish.

Answer these three simple questions:

- What is your purpose?
- What does your brand stand for?
- How can you show this in your product?

What might Giorgio say?

His purpose: to revolutionise, challenge and deconstruct tailoring, and as a result create a unique, timeless aesthetic for women and men.

What words might sum up what his brand stands for?

- Simple elegance and style
- Ease of movement through fabrics
- Confidence and attitude

How does that show up in his work?

- Deconstructed tailoring
- Beautiful Italian fabrics
- Subdued and unusual colours

I recently asked a brand owner what her biggest challenge was. She replied that it was lack of sales and that all she needed was a better sales person. When I dug deeper, she revealed that she found it hard to get the value of her collection across – buyers 'just don't get it'. How powerful could her brand be if she harnessed its uniqueness and articulated it well? Without that, she will continue to struggle.

This may sound a bit airy-fairy, but there's a practical reason to know your brand. You'll be clear about who you are today, what you stand for and how your product demonstrates this.

Back In 2000, a fashion journalist by the name of Natalie Massenet told me of a new venture she was launching. While we wandered the streets of Milan during fashion week she told me she was setting up a magazine-style ecommerce platform for high-end fashion labels, and that year Net-a-Porter was born.

In 2002, when I began to stock my Yulan collection on the site, there were around eighty brands on Net-a-Porter and I was the *only one under the letter Y. It was an incredible success, and in 2015 Natalie exited the company when it was valued at $2.2 billion and was merged with the online discounter YOOX. With a simple concept, she became the woman who proved that customers would buy designer and luxury goods online. How quickly the landscape of digital fashion has changed.*

Today, Net-a-Porter showcases over 350 brands and it's still growing. YOOX boasts 3,500 brands and Matches over 400 designer brands.

> *'That's a lot of images, products, words and "brand visions" for any customer to absorb. Imagine the buyers who have to assess these brands each season. Couple that noise with an increasingly impatient and less indulgent audience and it's not difficult to see how a collection can get lost.'* [8]
>
> Lou Stoppard, writing in *Financial Times Weekend*

A brand with a single clear message can slice through the noise of competition. I ask clients, 'Can your brand be understood in just three simple words?'

CASE STUDY – RED COLLECTION

I launched my women's collection, Yulan, as a full, ready-to-wear collection complete with jersey and knitwear. While it was well received, subsequent seasons proved trickier for audiences to connect with.

On reflection, although it was a complete collection at launch, it had one very simple message – the colour red. Every item that season was the same specific shade of the colour (a huge technical achievement, as insiders will understand). It was a concept that was easily understood, and this simplicity gave buyers a way in to the collection.

If your message is too complex for you to describe quickly, then others will struggle, too. Unfortunately, if they struggle, they'll probably just move on, hoping to find something that connects more easily.

> *'Our message was a tailored approach to swim shorts. With a clear message, the customer can immediately start to understand what you're about. That razor-sharp direct message really helped us.'*
>
> Adam Brown, Founder and Creative Director, Orlebar Brown

It's most effective to distil the message to its essence. Strip away complexity, detail and garnish until you have an unambiguous, crystal-clear idea that is easy to convey and difficult to misunderstand.

CASE STUDY – MISSONI

Italian company Missoni has not wavered all these years in its core message: luxury space-dyed knitwear.

The amazing expertise of creating unique space-dyed yarns, developing new stitches with the knit technicians every season, yet creating a fashion collection that's current, has taken generations to perfect, and you can see that. It's a wonderful, colourful world to experience, and a pleasure to work with a brand where every detail counts and the message is so clear.

Every brand has the ability to distil its message to a simple one based on a true purpose which can succeed where complexity gets lost.

Let's look at a UK fashion brand that has successfully built a strong culture. The culture is the core of what makes the business show double-digit growth season to season while other brands flounder in a competitive retail environment. Mathew Dixon is currently the global managing director at Karen Harvey Consulting and has worked for the most highly regarded and established fashion recruitment firms in London. There is little he does not know about brand culture and building a great team, so I asked him about the success of Ted Baker.

> *'That's been quite challenging. They work people very hard; there are times where it has been a pretty forceful culture. It was floated very quickly so they had to please shareholders very quickly. But even with that, it's a very, very dynamic culture because they believe in the brand. Everything comes back to what the brand stands for. You need to understand and agree to that, so when someone joins your business they absolutely appreciate what your business culture is. Within the great brands of the world, whether it's ones of the last ten years or last fifty years, there is a certain way of doing things. Whatever the particular way is – make sure people buy into that.'*
>
> Mathew Dixon, Global Managing Director,
> Karen Harvey Consulting Group

An authentic story around you and your product gets the market talking and creates a lasting impression. Regardless of how amazing your collection is, you need to build authenticity into your brand to articulate the value and thought process that goes into that collection.

Let's get back to James and his T-shirts. James has had some success as he's using great fabrics and the quality is unusual. He is running around like crazy growing the business. He's selling well online, but not growing fast enough; he is keen to move production to another country to get better margin and access better pricing. He is so busy working that he is hoping that the product is good enough to sell itself. Let's hear James tell his back story. 'I travelled to Tokyo in early 2010 with my girlfriend. Her dad owns a textile company in Japan. I fell in love with the city, its modernity, the crazy technology, its rigorous, orderly nature combined with incredible heritage and history.

'Naomi and I visited her dad's factory and saw the most amazing fabrics and textiles. He showed me the whole process of how it's all produced. I'm not into fashion really, but it was so technical and quite beautiful.

'After we'd done the tour, we headed back to his office. While Naomi was chatting to her dad, I began looking around on his office desk. Among the samples there were swatches of amazing jersey fabrics.

'The handle of the Japanese jersey was something I hadn't experienced before, and I thought immediately that it was something unique. It was refined, but also really casual feeling. T-shirts are my uniform, and I'm particular about the T-shirts I wear and always on the lookout for the best ones.

'Naomi's dad said the fabric was new and in development, and suddenly I saw an opportunity. The concept of Brand X was born.'

So now we know more about James and his journey, let's experiment with the value of product story telling.

'I believe in wardrobe heroes, believe in quality for the long term,' says James. 'My T-shirts are the perfect combination of a studied contemporary fit and modern Japanese fabrics, with a handle and finish that's been developed bespoke for us. The jersey is a high twist cotton linen blend, lightweight, washable, breathable, and doesn't crush when packed.'

All of a sudden, the £85 is justified.

So here we have a story about where an idea came from and how to blend it with a journey and set of principles. James already had the product, but now he has connected with his customer, showing the value of the product through an authentic brand story.

QUICK EXERCISES

- What inspired you to start the company?
- What values do you strongly believe in?
- What is the purpose of your brand?
- What makes you the best person to deliver it?
- What links your personal story to your brand?

Benefits:

Most brands when asked what they do, can't answer clearly. Creating that bedrock of an Authentic Brand Message (ABM) means you are able to answer these questions with absolute conviction and clarity.

- Your message will be razor sharp and consistent
- It gives you and your team clarity
- It motivates you and your team to aim high and focus
- It builds strong foundations for your business and brand which give a lasting impression

Outcome:

You will be more visible and cut through the noise as you express your message externally. You'll connect with your own brand story, giving you and your team the confidence in your work to convey its value to others. A convincing pitch to convey your value quickly and easily will make the right people pay attention.

CHAPTER 4

Language

Ecommerce and communicating through digital have affected fashion in an intriguing way. Take, for example, a tailored black blazer in a wool mix gabardine. How are you able to communicate the value of those fabrics online? The fabric looks like any another black fabric from any other company.

Suddenly there is a shift to make sure that there are close-up shots of the weave, accompanied by descriptive words like *'lightweight'*, *'breathable'*, *'high twist'*, *'fine'*, *'blended'*. Now the qualities of the fabric manufacture are important to highlight. This begins your journey into your product storytelling, giving the customer another reason to buy.

Look at what's happening right now in the world of wholesale.

I spoke recently with fashion show producer Lee Lapthorne, who had a very interesting take on the future of trade shows and showcasing fashion. He said that with recent disruptions (like terrorist attacks) and fragmenting of the show schedules, buyers from boutiques are becoming less willing to travel internationally.

How then do designers showcase their collections if they can't do so in person? Technology is where we will see leaps ahead, especially in how fashion brands reach out and communicate with buyers. While fashion shows will always have a place, look books and traditional photography will be soon be replaced with detailed rotating shots, augmented and virtual reality and film.

The shows already stream in real time. Future buyers will be able to access a whole array of tools and buy collections without the trouble of leaving their office.

> ' Moving images are where we're heading. Film, moving images, short film, GIF. You can leverage digital with film quite a lot. That's what we are focusing on at TANK. Video look books are interesting. Vogue now puts in each catwalk look as a video. Film – it's the new challenge.'
>
> Caroline Issa, Fashion Director and CEO of Tank

As digital is becoming the way in which fashion is communicated, it underlines that the future of storytelling will not just be around the authentic brand message, but also the evolution of language through which value can be transmitted.

> 'Another thing to notice is that attention to detail is changing to be more diverse and people want in-depth knowledge of the product itself and how the stitching and fabric are done. For

others it's about where the product comes from, who made it and has the whole production process been fairly, properly, consciously and sustainably developed.'

Andrea Ciccoli, Co-founder of The Level Group

James is back, and he's thinking about giving up his other job as a photographer. His T-shirts are selling fast, and he's working out whether to introduce other categories. He's super-ambitious and wants to make his mark, confident he can gain traction. He's passionate about showing that he can expand his collection successfully, but needs to work out what he wants to be known for. He thinks hard about his brand, and wants creative clarity in order to know how and when to extend the range.

James kept his brand's image minimal from the outset. With just one product, being minimal is not difficult. But he now wants to introduce more products, choice and complexity. He knows he must do this if he wants to grow the business.

How can he increase the range without diluting his brand?

With an authentic story already in place, brands that are successful need a distinct visual handwriting that is easily recognised. If you were gto look at a piece of clothing without branding from Missoni, it would be instantly recognisable. Same with a Dries van Noten blouse or Mary Katrantzou dress – you'd recognise them.

This does not happen organically or by chance. This distinctness, this visual language is the manifestation of a brand's values. It's something brands work out early on, and over time it is fine tuned into something exceptional.

'*Take for example Dries van Noten. Someone could set a colour palette down in front of you and you would say that's Dries. Same with Armani, you know what his brand stands for and what to expect. The key, I would say, is it's all about being you, creating what your product is, having your themes that are revisited, but emerging with that.*'

Barry Woods, Managing Director, Life Fashion Recruitment

A recognisable and consistent visual language on all platforms is vital to the customer experience and key to a long-lasting fashion business. Your collection will appear and sell on a range of different platforms so it's crucial that you establish and safeguard the visual integrity of your brand.

Larger businesses create detailed brand books that nail down every aspect of the history, vision, personality and key values of their brand. It's time to work out how your purpose and authentic brand story show up.

Building a distinct visual language

Have your ever noticed that a lot of UK brands seem pretty similar? The UK retail sector is suffering particularly. In my opinion, this is because it has become too generic, and the brands all tend to merge into one.

Competition in the UK is fierce, retailers have resorted to heavy discounts and markdown, which erodes further any trust customers had in the brand. Additionally, many of the mid-market UK retailers use the same factories and fabrics, picking from the same colour cards and using the same print suppliers. They operate on a system which is the opposite of design-led, and are buying the stock to past behaviour rather than looking ahead. This represents a perfect opportunity for new brands to deliver the extraordinary. That new brand could be yours.

Building a distinct visual language for your brand can be broken into five elements. Let's take each one in turn.

'What makes a brand authentic is when its own unique proposition is strong enough to be consistently communicated across all mediums and touchpoints. The key is to create a genuine identity and recognisable personality which lives beyond the product itself.'

Ruby Victor, Marketing Consultant

The five key areas of visual language are:

- Branding
- Fabrics
- Colour and pattern
- Silhouette and fit
- Image and photography

Branding. Having identified your Authentic Brand Message, you should find it easy to align branding with your story. Let's see how it worked for Petit Tribe, a childrenswear brand.

A few years ago, I was asked by a Nigerian entrepreneur to create a luxury childrenswear brand. Her family story and inspiration were irresistible and her smile and enthusiasm infectious. There was something really quite charming about the idea, so I agreed.

Before we began, we had many meetings, talking about her culture, background, life stories. She brought me fabrics and textiles from Africa, and described her childhood watching the Fulani tribespeople and the way they dressed. We talked about her aims for the brand and what she wanted to show through the collection. This key process created a vivid mental picture. Interpretation of that vision started with a full series of concept/brand boards. This initial exercise is important as it double-checks that the direction in my head matches my client's vision.

I knew that my client's ultimate aim was to pitch her brand to big department stores all over the world, so we looked at the competition and what they were doing. Instead of emulating them, I decided to look at womenswear branding instead. My client also emphasised that she wanted the brand to be a luxury experience for the shopper.

For the branding look and feel, I took it back to basics and looked at logo fonts in adverts, how they were cropped, the space around them, the colours. This was a great starting point, and I soon knew I'd create something white, clean and crisp for the branding. The collection was going to be colourful and rich, with the print of the collection an explosion of colour against that clean backdrop.

This is an example of how to bring values into a brand concept early on. Indeed, the contrast between a clean, modern look against a crazy African-inspired print made the concept stand out from the start.

This core work created a distinct visual language – touchpoints that became the foundation of the brand. The visual language became woven into the business pitch we put together to find suppliers and bring a high-level team together. To my client's amazement, doors opened up and everyone agreed to come on board.

'Successful fashion houses understand that a brand is essentially a symbol with a wider cultural context or 'world' that it represents, through its visual language and references.'
Ruby Victor, Marketing Consultant

Fabrics. What your brand feels like is very much part of your story. And I'm not just talking about emotions. Fabrics and materials are the building blocks of your product and opportunities for you to differentiate your brand from the rest. Take time and effort to study fabrics and work closely with mills to develop fabrics unique to you and your brand.

Giorgio Armani's research into fabrics is incredible, and I was exposed to his expertise early in my career. By the time I'd completed a few seasons, I could look with confidence through a collection of black crepes and pick out the winner, or pick through thousands of variations of micro-woven texture and soft tailoring gabardines. I find the research of the building blocks of fashion so exciting, and, working closely with mills to create bespoke fabrics, I take it a step further.

When I was working with Armani on the very first 'resort' collection for Collezioni, I worked out what I wanted the fabrics to look and feel like and then contacted the mills to ask them to create this, using blends of unusual fibres. They took a few weeks to trial and swatch and amend, but for the first season that I presented in New York, many of the fabrics were bespoke and totally unique to the market.

I'm incredibly passionate about pushing the boundaries of textiles, and am amazed that there are companies that don't spend time or expertise researching fabrics well. The opportunity is there for your brand to take the lead.

You may identify with Clare Hornby of ME+EM. Clare was

frustrated that she could not get her collection to the level she imagined in her head. One major sticking point was fabrics. In the first six months we worked together, I was listening and gauging whether she was ready for change. When we decided that we'd work together on the long-term project, I introduced her to a whole new world of fabrics.

Clare's brand has since formed great relationships with high-level mills which have transformed her business and were pivotal to the formation of the DNA of the brand. In harnessing this insider knowledge, Clare is now able to say she offers value to the customer and has something authentic. This knowledge made hers one of the only mid-range ecommerce companies using such high-level fabrics at that price point in the market. Clare now frequently talks in the press about fabric quality and research when speaking about the success of the brand. Just like me she's now hooked on getting fabrics just right.

'After working with you, I caught that obsession with fabrics and I go absolutely crazy when we get one wrong, for example if it creases too much or perhaps doesn't wash properly. I'm so mad because we might have let down hundreds of customers. Gaining customer trust comes down to recognising the issue and getting rid of it, then going back to the customer and making sure they know you care, and being transparent. It's not about waiting for them to be unhappy.'
Clare Hornby, Creative Director and Founder, ME+EM

So, if you want to stand out do your fabric research. Really push hard; don't be lazy. Go and search for the best fabrics in the category that you want to own. See what's happening in the market, what is pushing the boundaries.

'*Designers get rid of fabrics very quickly, which is insane. If you've found, for example, a good wool one season and it's sold well, then even if you don't want the same model back the following season, keep the fabric.*'

Marcia Ann Lazar, Founder and Managing Director, Zedonk

Colour and pattern. Your choice of colour can set your brand apart. If you continually pick from supplier colour cards and don't work on your own colour language then you will find over time that people will notice they can get the same colour in another brand.

Whatever your message is, how you present yourself through colour, how you style colours together, is important. Colour language is also a way to differentiate your brand and express your principles. Over time you can own the original and unique combination of colours.

The world of colour is a world of inventiveness and creativity. There are many millions of variations of colours, and if you study hard, work with the manufacturers and get your subtlety of colour beautifully correct, then that rigorous research will really pay off. Even though it might have been done before, if you stake your claim on a certain 'look' and consistently deliver it well, then sooner or later it will become yours.

In the *Financial Times* recently, journalist Mark C. O'Flaherty revealed the annual turnover at Agnès B was €290m last year. This has made Agnès Troublé one of the richest women in France. She is quoted as saying:

'*Since we launched, we've always sold the 12mm and 16mm striped tops, and we won't stop. It's a garment you know you can keep for ever. It works for children, men and women. Fashion is ephemeral. I have pictures of my clothes from 35 years ago, and they could have been taken last week.*[1]

Agnès Troublé

I love her statement. In today's crowded market, simple is good.

Caroline Issa has noted that with so many collections to see, a buyer's attention span is becoming shorter than ever.

' I've heard people don't look at the things in the showroom and just look at the tablet and say, "I'm going to take this because it sells best." That really frightens me.'

Caroline Issa, Fashion Director and CEO of Tank

What this means is brands need to articulate their message quickly and be consistent. Missoni, for example, created the art of space-dyed yarns. No one has any idea of the time and effort that the team goes to every single season to redevelop new colourways, but Missoni's complex and unique brand is extremely difficult to copy. Its colours give the brand a signature and DNA.

Have the confidence to build in core colours that become the mark of your brand.

'The major thing for any fashion label is brand identity, how to capture your DNA and hold on to it in an ever-changing industry.'

Lee Lapthorne, Creative Director and Founder, On|Off

Silhouette and fit. You need to identify how customers wear your clothes and the silhouette that they form. Fashion today is about style rather than a total look from a particular designer, which yet again is a result of so much product on offer. This means that customers like to pick and choose parts of an outfit, which means your task gets a little harder. Every item that they buy must deliver something of your brand DNA. Brands are now working out what customers feel when wearing their clothes. Do they feel flamboyant or confident? Stylish, sexy, professional, or contemporary? Perhaps the clothes are comfortable or the fit's flattering. Whatever the customer feels, it's become ever more important to understand what your collection and brand delivers when it is worn.

' Fit is another highly important factor, and very important for young designers. They might not have the technical abilities and they tend to be disconnected from their customers.'

Maria Lemos, Founder and Director of Rainbowwave

The fit of garments across brands is very different. Fit is a defining trait that again is a potential niche area for you.

For example, if you are at designer level, you are likely to be working to a slimmer and more European fit. You'll have higher underarms, narrower shoulders and longer arm lengths. If, on the other hand, you are working with different markets, you might be using a standard or more generous fit.

Make it your business to own a fit and silhouette. The pattern 'blocks' you create for your business are what you can develop and own and form part of your fit and shape language. That process gains you clarity so you can niche the customer, and the customer is going to buy your brand because of that unique factor.

Image and photography.

'Make sure your ecommerce photography and styling are the best they can be. Good photography sells product.'

Niki Brodie, Fashion Stylist and Consultant

In the age of digital and ecommerce, photography has become the medium of choice. There is a direct correlation between the quality of the photography and what sells. There's a balance, then. It's got to be 'on brand' yet it has to show the product.

If you look at the photography online for fashion brands, backdrops and poses are becoming more editorial in style. They are images that are created for multiple use.

Language through photography is one of the areas of brand building that I love. Much like finding the best manufacturer, finding a photographer who understands your brand and your authentic message is something you undertake with care.

For Petit Tribe, I chose a photographer named Julia Bostock. I'd been looking at her work since the beginning of the project, and her use of light and feeling for texture really swung my decision her way. We immediately bonded as she was working completely on my wavelength, and when I showed her the brand boards and explained the concept, she was hooked.

Although it took some months before we actually scheduled the first shoot, we remained in touch. It was the beginning of a key relationship for that brand.

Getting another creative to recognise what your brand stands for is a process. It's about building a strong link and nurturing that connection to produce the best results. Then they grow with you and your brand.

Once on board, Julia became part of the Petit Tribe family. My intuition paid off, and her photography of our prints made our social media campaign really stand out – so much so it got us noticed by *Vogue Italia* and we became the first ever children's brand to win their New Talent award in 2016.

James and Brand X

Let's talk through James's thought process and what he pulls together for his boards. James began with pretty minimal branding and the website he set up was equally simple. He's outgrown it already and is looking to launch a new one next season.

His authentic brand message is: 'Brand X, intelligent basics for every day and always.'

Branding. James keeps his branding clean with white space around it. He's keen to bring other elements of the manufacturing process into the branding so he refers back to the Japanese fabric. He pulls images of things he's seen on his numerous trips to Japan: leather cords, ceramic work, and weaving.

He's worked out that his new branding will incorporate both modern and old Japan.

Fabrics. The fabric board is covered in swatches of fabric, and photos from his trips to Japan inspire James. There's so much to choose from. James knows his core fabric is his signature jersey blend. He then moves to work out what complementary fabrics and new developments he can introduce. He blends the group of fabrics together in a rich story. What can he action now? What will he keep for later? What will be new for the season?

His promise is that the fabrics are light, washable, don't crush and are easy to pack. He's making sure everything on his board passes the Brand X test.

Colour and patterns. The Japanese mix of sharp lines inspires him, the fast-paced living contrasting with arts and crafts. Elegant, but relevant. James chooses to avoid stripes, using a more angular graphic jacquard motif and developing it in different scales. His colour palette contains deep black, washed greys mixed with stunning blues inspired by the hand-ground pigments in Japanese paintings. These are all Brand X signatures.

Silhouette and fit. James is a fit maniac and had stored a library of T-shirts prior to starting the brand, so he knew what he wanted. Not being a designer, he hired a consultant with design skills to help him develop three perfect T-blocks. James called them Aaron (classic crew), Alex (scoop neck) and Adam (raglan) after his friends. The T-shirts are super flattering. At the start, he was clever and worked closely with the garment tech and consultant to achieve the exact fit he wanted, then got his friends to test it and feed back. It's been a real labour of love.

A year in now, one style still has issues, but two are perfect and the returns are high. James has work to do and a decision to make whether to persevere or drop that fit.

He's now developing a jeans block and two shirt blocks. How can he interpret the language of his fit to the jeans and shirts? He's researching to make sure he continues delivering.

Image and photography. James is a photographer, but has never before worked on styling, so the first few shoots were a learning process. He made mistakes, but it all worked out fairly well. Having learned valuable lessons, he's investing in a proper team to do the next shoot. The Japanese aesthetic stops with the product, and he takes the photography in a different direction. He's keen to make it quite Californian in feel, shooting at his friend's mid-century house in LA which is angular, with 70s artwork and furniture. His look books and shoots will always incorporate an element of inside/outside lifestyle, and the colours are slightly faded or tinted. He's creating a look that he wants to be known for.

James has been shrewd. *He is going slow to go fast.* Instead of leaping off and developing a whole collection, he has taken time to gain creative clarity across the visual touch points of his brand before expanding. His business, even though it's small, is looking serious and well thought through. His distinct story interprets beautifully into a rich visual language. He is working on physical boards so he can show his message to his team and visitors to the studio. He has built strong foundations and guidelines. All of these are components of a fashion brand.

QUICK EXERCISES

- Are the visual touch points of your brand consistent?
- What key elements make it instantly recognisable?
- What makes it unique or distinctive from others?
- What key words describe what your customer feels?
- What links all your visual language to your brand story?

This work is the backbone of building strong brand visual guidelines. It will help drive better results working with your internal and external teams and create a distinct identity for your customers.

Benefits:

- It brings everything back into focus
- It clarifies your visual output and language
- It creates strong brand guidelines
- It strengthens distinctive visual touch points
- It highlights inconsistencies in the brand vision

Outcome:

The strength of creative vision and its consistency builds authority and credibility behind your brand. Linking this to your personal values makes it true and authentic. Many brands lack this creative confidence so getting this right will make you stand out.

CHAPTER 5

Innovation

James has come back from Japan very excited. He has found out that the new jersey fabric he's been developing is a better version of the last, and the process it goes through gives it a unique handle that's never been seen on the market before. He has also learned about an innovative fabric that can change temperature. That's given him some ideas. Could this fabric be combined with natural fibres to create something unique?

His current customers love his graphics and have been in contact on social media to ask for products with different colours and sizes. They want more. So James's brain has gone into overdrive, thinking about the exciting possibilities of the new technologies in Japan. He is thrilled and a little worried about the impatient calls from customers on social media, and hopes his competitors don't see these opportunities before he can act.

Should he explore these new possibilities or should he press pause, consolidate his market and refine his brand?

Fashion is ever-changing. The stock market drops and so do hemlines. Heated global political debates influence the appearance of slogans and religious motifs on the catwalk. Market uncertainty heralds the return of vintage clothing. New generations of customers rebel against big brands and find their own unique style.

Armani said recently that he loves the fashion business because it is intertwined with how we live and reflects what's important to us as a generation at any given moment. Digital has made fashion more connected and fluid than ever, and it's this that makes it so exciting. It's why people like James choose to be in this business. However, as fashion doesn't stay the same all the time, we need to be alert and attuned to what's happening, what's influencing it, and what direction it is being pushed in.

A new perspective on innovation

The biggest headache for the fashion business today is staying relevant, and relevance comes from investing in research, development and innovation. When I talk with clients about innovation, and test them to see if they are ready to think outside their comfort zone, many get quite anxious. They link the word 'innovation' to technology. If they have an artisan luxury brand, they can't see how innovation can relate to them.

I was recently invited to attend the FutureTech conference in Berlin, where new innovations that will appear over the next few years were being showcased. I was amazed what technology awaits us, and how it will be integrated into fashion. There were many examples, from smart textiles that will monitor our health, to fully connected garments that will have much of the functionality of mobile devices. LED lighting and conductive silver threads can be worked into textiles. The next big revolution will be the dawn of AR (augmented reality) and VR (virtual reality) into retail.

> *'It's not just new brands that are looking to leverage innovation. Established luxury brands too are looking for ways to remain relevant in the market. For example, Italian menswear brand Zegna has already been experimenting with a wearable tech for the last few years. Ferragamo have created a range of clothes made from fabrics created from recycled bi-products from orange peel.[1] We are only at the start of the integration of technology with fashion.'*
>
> Jo Ellison, Fashion Journalist, *Financial Times*

However, many brands fail to see its importance. It hit home to me that perhaps there exists a big gap in the perception of what innovation really means. Let me assure you that this is all part of the digital revolution and its effects are coming your way.

Innovation takes many forms. It can be applied not just to your product, but also across the business.

> *'You can't ignore innovation: be it how your warehousing works or how your website operates and the speed you can get the customer to the end basket. Innovation affects each part of the business.'*
>
> Adam Brown, Founder and Creative Director, Orlebar Brown

To begin with, I ask clients to do a complete, up-to-date competitor analysis, studying product, position and price to help them know rather than think they are offering something unique. This uniqueness must be beautifully aligned with the message and values of the brand.

> '*The value used to be based on price, quality and style. Now it's price, quality, style and story. It's a broader perspective than it used to be, which should be working in favour of a small business, as that's what they are focused on delivering.*'
> Andrea Ciccoli, Co-founder of The Level Group

Let's break the innovation process down into four key parts:

- Niche
- Unique in context
- Innovate in your sector
- Best in class

Niche your product

As designers, we tend to think in terms of collections, yet the experts I spoke to for this book all agreed that niche is the way forward, unless you have the budget of a large retail or luxury company. Is yours the best little black dress, or the best striped T-shirt? Humble items can be the foundation of a great brand.

Editing what you can do, producing a single extraordinary item, is a challenge, but it's necessary to cut through the noise in a crowded market. Your item will be the one that fits clearly with your brand message and visual language.

> '*Those that are growing their niche or one product category with a strong brand identity are doing well. It's just much*

easier for customers to understand. Otherwise, the message gets confusing.'

Maria Lemos, Founder and Director of Rainbowwave

Many designers like myself have been in that position. We believed that to be taken seriously, we had to show a complete collection; total looks, as it were, including woven, knits, jersey, even leather or accessories. Today's market requires something else. Customers have moved on.

CASE STUDY – YULAN

I launched my brand Yulan from the perspective of a creative (me) wanting to express my aesthetic point of view. That seems naïve now, but fifteen years ago the digital age had only just begun.

I had carried out a little basic market research. I saw my brand sitting alongside Jil Sander and other well-known brands. My target wholesale accounts were the same as theirs.

The first collection was meant to have been a 'pilot' and not for sale. However, the pilot launch went so well I made the decision to take orders and effectively 'pushed the button'.

Of course, I was completely thrilled to get my brand launched and into arguably the best-known showrooms in London and Milan, and to get orders from the big stores in my first season. But it was one of the worst decisions I ever made.

I had done my price structure, but it was not based on reality. I could not sustain delivery of my collection at that quality and at that price. It was the wrong moment and I was unprepared. It set the clock ticking for me to organise my studio, my production and myself.

If I'd done the research, I would have understood the fundamentals of costings and production as a small brand. I was using the best fabrics and mills yet producing low quantities – never a winning combination if you are trying to make your collection sit in line with those of competitors. More importantly, I did not have a clear enough edge above the competition in the market at that time.

Cash flow and production became big issues that resulted in closure after four years. If I had taken the time to examine the market and my competitors, I may well have adjusted my collection to be more focused and far less complex. I had stretched myself too thinly by breaking into a range of categories instead of just one.

If I'd had a clear understanding of my USP from the start, things might have turned out quite differently.

Perhaps the biggest lesson to learn from my experience is that the energy and resources to develop full collections for independents are simply unaffordable and unsustainable. Graeme Black launched his eponymous luxury label, only to suffer from the same issues.

'My collection was too big, too dispersive, it wasn't focused enough and was very expensive to produce. It was a huge collection, far too complex. In hindsight that's what attracted people, but equally what confused people. I had some very good advice from a couple of buyers who came in and said, "Oh you know, I love your leather, I love your jersey, just do that", but I didn't listen to them when I should have.

'It was very difficult to deliver. The deliveries of many different factories meant delivering at different times and consignments into stores were impossible to manage at the same time.

'If I were to launch my label again, I would do just one product category, and concentrate on that. And be known

for that. Understand the price point of that. That's what's working today.'

Graeme Black, Creative Director and Owner, Graeme Black

Don't underestimate the massive upside to niching your collection. It helps you focus your range and therefore increases the numbers you order in one category from a smaller number of suppliers, which in turn makes your relationships with suppliers closer. It fine-tunes the product as less time is wasted developing styles that are unnecessary, and ultimately gets you better prices and better delivery. Everything seems easier.

Niche your market

Entrepreneur Luca Marini launched Finery, a British contemporary fashion label, in 2014. He serves the high street market but has created buzz with a revised business model.

Finery is a great example of how to get it right when it comes to a laser focus on a niche, but it's not a product, it's an age group. Marini worked out that the twenty-five to thirty-five age group was looking for a unique designer look, colourful and original but at an accessible price. He has blended the UK retail structure with a high level of creative talent, letting his team and designers push the boundaries and experiment. It's a breath of fresh air.

Finery shows many styles, sees what the reaction is and responds quickly to the demand, much like the model of ASOS. Marini's pricing strategy and business structure are possible because they were planned meticulously before he began.

When *Drapers Magazine* interviewed him recently it revealed just how organised and detailed he is.

'*At Finery, Luca supervises all operations, including warehousing, logistics, customer care and payments. Finery had an exceptional first year of trading, with over £5m in revenues and 3m visits to its website in 2015. Product without good* [operational] *execution is nothing.*' [2]

Interview with Luca Marini, Co-founder and Chief
Operating Officer, Finery London, in *Drapers Magazine*

Unique in context

Competitor analysis and market research are key parts of business planning. Doing your homework about your competitors and the market will please future investors and put your mind at ease.

If you are struggling to grow your company, it is likely that you have too much competition in your market sector. You may have the right product but not at the correct price. You may have both product and price right, but are not be reaching the right customer.

The context of your brand – where it's placed in a store, what brands it sits next to – will reflect your overall message. This context must be aligned with your business goals and what you want to say.

All too often brands will launch and muddle through a pricing strategy, thinking of the short term but failing to look at the business in the long term. It is a numbers game during the growth years, and it's common for growing brands to struggle to reach the minimums for the suppliers they want to work with. If you are not clear from the outset where you and your product sit, you will likely suffer from one of two common issues.

Issue one – you launch your brand at a benchmarked, competitive price. It sells, but you make no margin.

Issue two – you price your brand according to the margin you'd like to make and it ends up perceived as too expensive and has low sales.

If you benchmark yourself alongside big well-established brands, remember that they are producing larger quantities than you will be able to achieve in the first three years.

The result of both scenarios is that at best your business will always struggle to gain traction, or at worst you will go bankrupt – unless you have deep pockets to fund the business over at least three years and are playing a long-term price strategy, or you're thinking about how to add value to your product to merit a higher price.

Innovate in your sector

Many younger businesses are savvy enough to realise they must have a point of difference. Many have even cottoned on to manufacture and materials as the way to build value into their brand. However, many launch their brand without making sure its foundations are watertight.

'*How do you become unique in the market place? Many people who contact me think our USP is simply "Made in Britain", but it takes much more to make a fantastic product.*'
Kate Hills, Founder of Make It British

The uniqueness of product, fashion and technology enables companies to create one-off designs. From my experience, the companies doing well are offering the masses customised products, which in most cases needs to be done locally.

You may struggle to see how your business can innovate, but it is possible. Let's look at how the new generation of creatives are thinking differently about everything.

'*The new generation naturally challenges the norm. It is simply ingrained into their mentality. Look at what the tech business is currently doing within our sector – they are not as emotionally connected to the fashion cycle. They see different ways we could reach many more people by changing the way we look or sell things.*'

Mathew Dixon, Global Managing Director,
Karen Harvey Consulting Group

The industry to date has been shackled to an archaic calendar and driven by a self-perpetuating wheel. The whole industry – the brands, press and buyers – all worked according to the cycle, but something had to change, in particular with small brands, where cash flow is the biggest challenge.

Before now, few in the industry would dare challenge the well-established structure of the show. There was a fear that if you said no, you'd be turned down. Yet now brands are jumping to explore alternatives. Somebody had to do it and people realised the logic in it.

Look for opportunities to challenge the norm and do something differently. It's less about broadening your product and more about improving and refining what you already have. Move forward in line with the market.

Innovation might come through new fabric developments. It might come through the way you produce. It might come through your use of technology and imagery, or from how you deliver your product.

Let's look at two examples of the movers and shakers who

are approaching business in an innovative way. The first is Everlane, a San Francisco-based entrepreneurial-led clothing brand that's managed to innovate through disrupting the production cycle.

With a promise of 'Modern basics, Radical transparency', Everlane made it its mission to make all production costs transparent, to streamline the process and pass that saving onto the customer. Unlike other players in their market, they keep inventory very tight, reordering the popular items when needed. That means they never put their put their products on sale and customers have to actually wait while items are restocked. It's a winning business strategy, keeping inventory risk low, forging tight collaborations with suppliers, changing the dynamic of cash flow yet not compromising the quality, whilst keeping brand perception high. This genius innovation has helped reach a company valuation of $250 million after only six years of business.[3]

Our second example of innovation in action comes from UK company Unmade, another entrepreneur-led business. Promising 'unique knitwear that redefines personal style', Unmade's USP is getting customers to engage though customisation, and then the company delivers bespoke complex jacquard knitwear to them within six to eight days.

These brands have challenged the production cycles and are carving a niche not through their product, but through their experience and its delivery. Both websites (as they are both ecommerce) clearly lay bare the process that the products go through. It's this sort of transparency that is greatly reassuring to customers. So ironically, they are using production chain disruption to add value and they pass that value to the customer. Although these brands are making their name as 'disruptors' of the fashion cycle, I see them as pioneers.

'They are not so much "disruptors" but they are coming from a non-traditional way of looking at things. I think what I love about Everlane is that they show clearly what the actual costs are. It's very transparent and direct.'

Caroline Issa, Fashion Director and CEO of Tank

Best in class

'Given there is such a huge revolution in the storytelling, it becomes more important to link story to product. It's a huge opportunity for new brands, which are dynamically able to get it and get it across.'

Andrea Ciccoli, Co-founder of The Level Group

I was walking around a trade fair in Berlin the other day and came across two brands. Both were collections from Italy and both were selling coats, but I could not believe how different they were.

Brand One had a rather beautiful bright white stand, which had attracted my attention as it was raised. I had to climb up a staircase to get to it. The staircase was curiously lined with novels.

It became evident that the clothes were outerwear, but instead of being displayed on hangers, they were hooked up singly with plenty of space around them, back lit, and framed by photographs of nature and the outdoors. There was a cheerful chap on the stand. When I asked him to tell me a little about the collection, he gave me his full attention.

'It's a unique collection,' he explained, 'in that the fabrics used, while they look like fashion fabrics, are treated then bonded with Lycra, transforming them into performance materials.'

He then took what looked like a regular woman's coat made from a woven wool material with a textured surface and turned it inside out, showing me how it had been bonded to a performance neoprene. It was totally waterproof. The seams inside were all bonded together, and not only that, there were various layers that detached and could be worn separately. The men's coats could be manipulated in the same way.

'These are fashion garments made for adventure and travel,' he said, excited to talk about the collection. I was so intrigued, I spent a good half an hour with him and ended up interviewing him for this book.

Brand Two, in contrast, had a stand around the corner. This stand consisted of three rails of hanging garments and one rather despondent sales representative sitting at a desk. Apart from a large and dated logo above the rail, no attempt at branding had been made at all. It was so incredibly uninviting that I did not even look at the clothes, but I did make the time to chat with the sales representative.

It turned out that the product was not only Italian, but beautifully made by a company with a rich outerwear background. Yet the company had not even briefed its sales team. There were neither visual tools nor stories to engage with the customer. The representative had been armed with nothing but a rail of clothes and a price list.

She revealed that the owner did not care for storytelling, nor explaining too much. In fact, the owner believed the collection was so strong it would sell itself.

What a stark difference between two companies. One was forward thinking, the other stuck in the past. It's no surprise to hear from the organisers of the trade fair that some brands complained that they did not have much interest, while others in the same category, with the same size of booth, same origins, same quality, did incredibly well.

I asked Riccardo from (Brand One) RRD Italy what it takes to make a brand engaging.

'Storytelling is fundamental. In fact, we call our garments "stories". Each one has a story that needs to be told. Customers are spoilt for choice, and already have everything. Now people are looking for stories that they can believe in and recognise themselves from.'

He also agreed innovation, staying ahead of the curve, and aiming to be the best in class are crucial.

'If you are a small company, you can't stay on the same garments, same size and kind of products for many years. You have to innovate continuously and propose new concept, new styles, and new fabrics in the market. That's why one of our mottos is constant research and development. That's the key of innovation.'

Riccardo Guidati, Business Development Coordinator, RRD

This is why, when I work with clients, I constantly push them to keep going, aiming high, especially when it comes to product. They find it tough as I'm such a stickler for detail, but as my training has taught me, and as you can see from the above examples, attention to detail can get you noticed.

CASE STUDY - ME+EM

Let me tell you the story of a design that I created for ME+EM. When we first met, owner Clare had often said that she'd like to own stripes. She comes from a marketing background and knew what she wanted, so I set about creating Britain's best striped T-shirt.

After a huge and laborious process, the Breton T was launched. On the surface and in photography, this little T-shirt might not have looked any different to many others, but I'd designed nine details into the garment to make it stand out.

A slash neckline only suits certain people, and there was a lot of convincing to be done before Clare approved the neckline. The T-shirt has got little ruches at the waist that create a flattering movement. I made it ever so slightly longer than usual so that it does not pull up when the wearer is moving around. The slight envelope neck bindings give a little French touch. The fit has a perfect armhole yet does not restrict.

The exact stripe design took hours of deliberation and trials, but eventually we found a vintage sample which did the trick. The jersey fabric – should we do plain jersey or 1 × 1 rib stitch? For those who don't know the terminology, the difference is in the hand feel, and we opted for the latter as it's softer. Optic white or natural white; cobalt or navy? Questions and colour combinations can take weeks in a design-led business.

Then the name. I've always loved J-P Gaultier's signature striped Ts, hence the Breton was born.

It was this simple T-shirt that Kate Middleton, Duchess of Cambridge, chose to wear on the first day of her tour of New Zealand in 2014. Kate featured on the cover of every newspaper the following day, often in double page spreads, glowing and smiling gloriously on a speedboat, and 'The Breton T-shirt from unknown British brand ME+EM' sold out immediately. It is now a brand asset and IP and is unique to ME+EM.

It just goes to show that even a striped T-shirt can be original, and three years on Clare can say with confidence she now owns stripes.

Distinguish yourself from your many competitors. Find and exploit your niche by researching and understanding your market before being clear about the distinctiveness of your offer. Be best in class; stay clear of the mediocre crowded middle ground by pushing boundaries and embracing innovation. Then use your distinctiveness to inspire confidence and authority for your business.

Last time we saw James, he had come back from Japan filled with ideas and presented with opportunities to expand. Is he ready?

In Japan, he discovered that the fabric used in his T-shirt is patentable. His future father-in-law (did I mention that he got engaged to Naomi?) offers to pay for the patent as a gift. And now it's truly unique to James's brand.

With one patent to his name, he's decided to explore innovative fabrics further. So, for next season he has asked another factory in Japan to work on combining a fabric that can change temperature with natural fibres.

He can't ignore his current customers, so he's put out a call to them online to compete to pick the new colour to add to the collection next season. The winner will get a unique bespoke graphic piece in the new jacquard pattern.

The *Financial Times*'s 'How to Spend It' supplement has expressed an interest in covering new innovative men's brands, so James will also do a bespoke piece for the editorial.

James is progressing fast. He's sharp and knows he has to do what he can to stay ahead of the curve. There is a lot of competition, so in order to keep having something fresh to recruit new customers and interest the press, he has to innovate and offer the unique. He understands he has to engage with customers.

QUICK EXERCISES

- What one product, service or process you are known for?
- What makes it best in class?
- What brand is the nearest competitor?
- What issue do you solve better than they do?
- What future innovation is relevant to your business?

It's no longer enough to be a talented designer or creative entrepreneur. In today's fast-paced environment research, development and innovation is where you will truly differentiate your brand, and what makes the ordinary exceptional.

Benefits:

- It uncovers your unique point of difference
- It identifies and strengthens the core of your fashion business
- It researches and stakes your claim to your market
- It makes steps to innovate and create IP value
- It gives you the confidence you are offering the exceptional

Outcome:

Investing in research and development will mean you are always one step ahead of the curve, and remain a relevant brand. Embracing innovation and developments in your sector means you can always have an edge and confidence to know rather than think you are unique.

Gain Trust

James's brand has now gathered some die-hard fans – customers who buy from him again and again. Every now and then he gets emails or feedback, some so great he has been thinking of using them as testimonials.

Some customers, however, don't come back. The ecommerce returns have remained within normal parameters, but it still bothers him that something is causing customers concern. As we know, James is into the detail of his product, driven to eradicate any issues and keen to make sure customers continue to love his brand.

James takes a bold decision. He explains his ethos, that he is driven to make sure customers are satisfied. Once he's made his promise, over a three-month period he asks his team to set up a channel where customers can feed back to a real person. He has one of the team placed on standby to answer any queries. He also sets up a channel to get customers to send photos and describe their issue. At the same time, he starts a proactive campaign – if anyone requests a refund or replacement, he pledges to have the issue resolved in forty-eight hours at no cost.

James and the team wait to see what happens next.

We have entered an extraordinary period of interconnectivity. We are communicating almost every second of every day. We pretty much know everything about everyone in real time.

This access to data has given enormous power to the consumer, who can share views and feedback, complain, return, recommend or reject at superfast speed. It has also opened up a whole new world of opportunity for fashion businesses if handled well.

Our American friends have taken this shift in power very seriously, and many brands have successfully taken back some control by actively participating in the never-ending sharing of information. 'Brand alignment' describes the art of communicating brand value to customers. Yet too few fashion companies look at the success of that strategy. They don't take the customer and their brand experience seriously enough.

'*Where you see real movement is in the companies that have really embraced digital. By this I don't mean just bringing on board a young hipster who sits in front of social media. I mean brands that have moved digital to being the heart of the business*'

Mathew Dixon, Global Managing Director,
Karen Harvey Consulting Group

'*Consumers align themselves with a company when they can recognize its brand promise and trust in its ability to keep that promise.*[1]'

Gallup Business Journal

Data is the new currency

With this direct-to-customer opportunity comes the under-standing that the customer is now in the driving seat. For a brand to succeed, it is obliged to pivot and change from the past mentality of transmitting and dictating to listening and understanding.

So as fashion turns to face the customer, technology is moving fast to improve the ability to gather and read huge amounts of data. It's so sophisticated that it knows everything about demographics – personal details of what we watch, what we eat, our buying habits, how frequently we shop. This data is there now, ready to be used to target marketing with laser precision.

'*We now have direct access to customers, so if you don't analyse that behaviour and if you don't engage with your customer and if you don't try to understand who they are as real people, then the brilliant advantage of digital is kind of pointless. Pay attention to what your customers are telling you and keep your customer first, always. It's now all about the customer. And I think if you know who that customer is and you have a vision to deliver something to them, then you are off to a strong start.*'

Paula Reed, Fashion and Brand Consultant

'Brands must not lose sight of the fact that the customer is still at the core. Digital is actually making the customer proposition easier as it is a broader, faster format which offers an integrated platform with a multitude of ways to merchandise product and engage with the customer – all with the end goal of delivering on the customer promise and the potential of exceeding the customers' expectations.'

Marty Wikstrom, Founder, Atelier Fund and Corporate Director

The winners in the game are of course the giants who have been gathering our data for years. Look at the likes of Amazon and Google. Whatever product they chose to create and launch would succeed because they hold so much data about us. They know us better than we know ourselves.

Ironically, despite the head-spinning amount of data available, we are still moved to buy through feelings, emotions and communication.

As we saw in Chapter 2, a brand must first have authenticity. You need to be clear about what your brand stands for and what it is that you do. Your challenge is to cut through all of the noise and communicate your value to your market.

'A business needs to have a point of difference. A strong point of view comes from a clearly defined vision and that is always invaluable. That's something that can't be replicated by a machine. It can't be created by an algorithm.'

Paula Reed, Fashion and Brand Consultant

In today's digital market you gain trust by:

- Solving a problem elegantly
- Being consistent and clear about what you stand for

- Understanding and engaging with your customers
- Being open and inclusive
- Delivering great customer experience/service

Solve a problem elegantly

It's crucial to understand that your product has a purpose and solves a problem for your customer. Whatever you design must function in the customer's wardrobe.

Be consistent and clear

> '*If employees do not understand their company's identity and what sets it apart, it is unlikely that customers will either. If employees do not have a clear idea of their company's brand promise, it is unlikely they will be able to deliver it to customers.*'[2]
>
> Gallup Poll

If, like James, you're confident that your offer is unique, you have defined your authentic brand message and visual language, now align the tone of voice and tell stories about your brand

> '*That message, that brand story is really important. We are all storytellers, we all love stories. We are looking for stories, information, insight and ideas and we are happy to share that. That's what content is. When it's done well it feels effortless. Take Burberry, for example. Their two-minute film on the trench was amazing. They build communities around products. They really know why they exist, who their customer is and how to talk to them.*'
>
> Rhodri Williams, Head of Business Development, Liberty Marketing

You may be clear on your brand message, but what about the people who work for you? Ensure that staff understand your message and are fully equipped to explain it to customers and clients.

> *'Everything comes back to what the brand stands for. Agree to it and understand it so when someone joins your business they will appreciate what your culture is. The great brands of the world over the last 10 years or 50 years know there is a way of doing things. Whatever it is, that is your way. Just make sure people buy into that.'*
> Mathew Dixon, Global Managing Director,
> Karen Harvey Consulting Group

Multibrand boutiques like to brief their staff as they know how important their people are in communicating brand message. Give staff more than a wordy press release about the 'inspiration' behind the collection – tell them the story with words and images so that they can transmit the value behind your brand.

CASE STUDY – ANGELA SCOTT

On a trip to LA, my friend and I were doing some retail research and were shopping in the Melrose district. We looked at the window of what appeared to be a new shoe store.

We popped our heads around the door and were greeted by a cheery hello. The shoes were great and very much my aesthetic: like brogues revisited. I turned the shoes over in my hand. They were well made – and, to my surprise, a product from Portugal.

The sales assistant approached and told us a great story. The lovely dove-tail effect on the heel was inspired by her father, a cabinet maker and carpenter. She showed us the unusual striped detail (technically very difficult to paint, she explained) running over the toe and following right under the shoe.

As I listened and browsed, I realised that not only had the brand wonderful details and a great story, but the cost was 25% less than I would have expected from a similar Italian label. This brand (at a retail level) hit the mark and the story was so charming that, for me, it delivered superb value.

Go to Angela's website where she'll ask you to sign up to 'join the family'. The word 'craftsmanship' sits firmly in the centre of the navigating bar. It's all part of the story, and for a small company, she's communicated the brand message very effectively.

'*Telling a story is a fundamental skill, which needs to be updated and revisited for the digital age. This means more product stories and shared stories rather than 'speakerphone' brand stories. Brands need to create community support and customer contribution to be developed.*'

Andrea Ciccoli, Co-founder of The Level Group

Sometimes brand value can be communicated with the simplest of descriptions. During those early years working with ME+EM, we often experimented with the words to describe leggings we had developed. The leggings were made with high-quality Italian gabardine that had been chosen for its matt finish and dry handle.

The primary selling point was that the fabric 'returned', i.e. it didn't go baggy once you'd worn it. The leggings were designed for comfort and to be practical – delivery of Italian fabric with an excellent fit and at a good price. All we needed were the words.

Some potential descriptions popped up, including the ultimate black legging and legging essential, but 'Leg Corsetry' was the inspired name we settled on. We added on the words 'leg lengthening' for maximum effect.

Needless to say, the seemingly simple black leggings were a huge success.

Then we experimented with our newly launched ruched dress and called it 'drop a dress size'. Here was another simple spin on words that articulated succinctly the solution for the customer.

However, customers don't want to be misled. The regular customers of a certain high street store felt a little disillusioned with the brand's markdown strategy. Customers love discounts, but after seeing a store advertising a special 30% sale, they won't love seeing a markdown of up to 50% on offer in the same store a few days later. This kind of promotion undermines trust. What will customers think the next time they see the store's 'special' sale? If they were fooled first time into acting swiftly, they may be more suspicious next time.

If customers detect that you are not telling the truth, their distrust leads to devaluation. Have you flip-flopped around markdown strategy? Address it quickly as it devalues your hard work and brand immensely.

Understand and engage with your customers

Over the last fifteen years, it has been enough to get an ecommerce platform up and running. These days, budgets are being re-allocated to data analysis and understanding how to engage.

Marketing and sales teams are working together with digital teams to bring brand messages clearly and precisely to the customers. Some companies invest a lot of money acquiring large numbers of followers in the hope that their time on Instagram and other social media platforms will convert into sales. It's not easy, and most businesses are still experimenting, looking for something that works.

> ' ...finding new customers who value the product for the right reasons. The speed that information moves can send business owners into a tizzy. There are so many platforms: figuring out your message across all those platforms can be overwhelming.
>
> 'It's going to be more important to know the quality not quantity of your database and social followers. If you don't know who the audience is, how engaged they are, then how can you convert your audience?'
>
> Caroline Issa, Fashion Director and CEO of Tank

So in marketing and communications, what works today? Print, digital, traditional advertising?

As we attempt to find a way to reach and engage customers directly through digital, the role of traditional PR and marketing strategy must also come under scrutiny. Neither traditional marketing nor digital in isolation performs in predictable, measurable ways anymore.

> ' I've been in meetings with brands and the marketing department just has a massive rant. They can spend millions on billboards or magazine adverts, but when it comes to the budget for a PPC campaign or Google ads they don't want to commit. They think of digital as being banner ads. They just don't get it.

'Digital and traditional marketing and PR can't be seen as separate. They are the same, and the end customer is the same. It does not matter how you communicate with them. Television, radio, magazines, social media, YouTube – they are just tools to connect with that person. It has to be embraced as one. It's all about understanding their behaviour.'

Rhodri Williams, Head of Business Development, Liberty Marketing

Matt Booker, owner of COUSIN, a UK printing company, believes that there is a balance, but no one has worked out the formula quite yet. That said, his business is on the up as brands are returning to physical marketing tools such as brochures and catalogues.

'There's an awful lot more thought to be put into combining digital and print effectively. Fashion businesses are starting to realise that there is a colossal cost to a lot of their digital activity. It does snowball at an incredible rate; you have to be on every social media channel; you have to shout out louder and faster than anyone else just to get heard. The better digital gets, the more important physical communications become as they can cut through this noise.'

Matt Booker, Founding Director of COUSIN

Physical print is by all accounts alive and well, and needs to be considered as part of your marketing mix. Printed product is less ephemeral than digital communications. As a new generation of music fans discover the tactile pleasures of vinyl over streaming, so too, are people perceiving the value of a printed item more than they were. Craftsmanship is becoming more and more appealing to people.

Printed products are used not only to keep a brand front of mind, but also to drive traffic to the website. For this reason alone, the printed brochure has a tangible return on investment.

In a recent survey, Royal Mail collected responses from households regarding the emotional impact of physical mail versus email. Here are the astounding results of three questions:

Did you take the mail seriously? Result: physical mail – 63% said yes compared to email's 18%.

Did you feel valued? Result: physical mail – 57% said yes compared to email's 17%.

Did it give you a better impression of the company? Result: physical mail – 55% said yes compared to email's 25%[3]
Source: Royal Mail MarketReach

Ecommerce brands looking to expand and take their business up a level are still considering investing in printed brochures. Print in fashion genuinely does offer a point of difference. A printed product that is well executed and planned has the capacity to tell a story that online doesn't.

The rapid and devastating disruption of traditional retail by digital is the subject of other books. But let's not give up on bricks and mortar just yet. A key takeaway from the research I carried out for this book is that there will always be a role for physical retail.

> ' The function of retail today is acquisition rather than retention. When the customers come to the store, we acquire the customer. The retail environment is a really good place to get them over the line and give them the confidence to purchase for the first time.'
> Adam Brown, Founder and Creative Director, Orlebar Brown

Creating a great ecommerce website might look easy, but to get it right demands time and investment.

> 'The mistake is to think that getting ecommerce right is something that's cheaply done. It's not cheaply done; it's a major investment. The benefit is you can tell your story, without the filter of anyone else's interpretation. If it is at all possible, try to remain as independent as you can be for as long as possible, because you can control your own platform and the investment that you make. And never, ever under any circumstances sell your name.'
> Paula Reed, Fashion and Brand Consultant

It's paramount then to communicate well on ecommerce. How to replicate the experience of shopping in a physical store is the biggest challenge for all brands. The retail outlet is the window to your brand and needs to be totally in line with all of your other output. The visual touch points of your branding need to be confirmed and strengthened for your customer.

> 'If anything, it's like opening a shop on the quietest street in the world. You can make your clothes and put them on the website, but you have to figure out how to create traffic and then conversions.'
> Adam Brown, Founder and Creative Director, Orlebar Brown

Ecommerce is just part of the buying journey. It's another place where customers come to experience you and your brand. How you engage with your customers offline is becoming increasingly important. Engage directly with clients with personal shopping events, exclusive shows and trunk shows. If you can get to meet real customers where they can give you feedback, grab the opportunity. It is invaluable.

' I love physically seeing a customer in the retail environment, being on the shop floor. Nothing beats talking to the customer and seeing their immediate reaction to your collection.

Adam Brown, Founder and Creative Director, Orlebar Brown

Additionally, as discussed in the previous chapter, customising products is another way to get the customer to invest in the transaction and value it more. Customisation is far from being a new idea. Ben Perkins, head of consumer business research, Deloitte, writes that the company was *'talking about personalized products being the next big thing in the 1970s, but only now do we have the technology to do it at scale.'*[4]

Nor does it require massive input from the customer. Simply choosing the piping trim on a pyjama print or the colour of leather on a handbag handle, the customer has made the transaction more personal and meaningful. Many brands have introduced this element of choice. It draws customers into an exchange, which in turn makes them perceive the value. Deloitte found that 71% of consumers interested in personalised products are prepared to pay a premium.[5] There is a strong case for letting shoppers take the design reins and add their personal touch to purchases.

Be open and inclusive

To build a long-lasting fashion brand, you must be able to create a loyal customer base. Customers who are happy with the product, your message and everything that your brand stands for will come back for more.

And more than that, your loyal customer will become an advocate for you. In fashion, word-of-mouth is more valuable than any advertising. Brand fans will pass on a message of a brand that has delivered.

Your customer experience wins brand fans from the moment they look at the website to the moment they receive your parcel through the post. It's no longer enough to pour more money into advertising and endorsements. In fact, this kind of spend may be wasteful.

' ...*these tactics simply promote a message; they do not deliver what consumers really value – an actively aligned brand promise. Consumers want to walk into a store, go online, or contact a customer care center and have the experience they were promised. They want companies to back up their taglines and follow through on their guarantees. When companies do this, consumers will align themselves with those brands – and ultimately, will trust them.*' [6]
Gallup Poll

'*Whatever you produce, it has to be authentic. If you are sending brochures, catalogues or look books, they must be in line with your campaign imagery and true to the products you're selling. Many brands cut corners at the last hurdle, and when they produce the brochure, the colours look terrible. For the customer, it's annoying when fashion looks great as an image, but when the product arrives it's a completely different colour. This feeling is the precise opposite to the excitement and anticipation everyone has worked so hard to generate. Trust is damaged and there's a wholly unnecessary cost generated when the product is returned.*'
Matt Booker, Founding Director of COUSIN

Brands that are retaining customers are those that are building communities. Orlebar Brown's website and social feed encourages customers to post photographs of themselves wearing their swim shorts. This type of engagement is not unusual, but customers can also create their own shorts by uploading their photographs. This kind of engagement makes customers feel that they are part of a family; that they and the brand share certain values.

> *'In a world where the big labels and super brands have such an emotional tug on the customer, we counteract this with the highest levels of personal service and attention to detail. Our customers return again and again because we build a common history. We know what they've had from one season to another and we understand their lifestyle. We amend and alter their patterns from season to season as their figures might change, ensuring easy fittings. Clients don't wish to spend hours having their clothes altered even when ordering bespoke items.'*
>
> Stewart Parvin, MVO, couturier

Deliver great customer experience

> *'I think it all comes down to outstanding customer service, which builds customer loyalty. Right from the outset, I wanted the customer to know that if they hand over £150 for a product, they'll be looked after.'*
>
> Adam Brown, Founder and Creative Director, Orlebar Brown

The customer experience of a brand from beginning to end has to be managed carefully. Many brands are just happy to fulfil their orders and move on to resolve other impending issues once the money is in the bank. To grow your business and to build loyal customers, you need to see the customer journey right the way through to the end.

Chatting to Clare Hornby of ME+EM she agreed that customer focus is crucial.

> *'Once you have a single-minded strategy, and deliver that, your customers begin to play it back to you. Once you set your strategy, you have to stay firmly on that track, because they are so incredibly discerning that the minute you change direction, they will spot it a mile away. If you can get them to play back the strategy to you, then you've achieved customer loyalty.'*
>
> Clare Hornby, Creative Director and Founder, ME+EM

CASE STUDY – THE WHITE COMPANY

A few years ago, the White Company contacted me. Chrissie Rucker and her team were looking to 'crack' clothing. They were already an established, successful ecommerce company with revenues of near £100m but they saw an opportunity and wanted to expand into new territory.

One of the many reasons why TWC is so hugely successful is its methodical approach to CRM (Customer Relations Management). This company is a great example of a lifestyle brand that's managed to branch into fashion because it had already built up customer trust.

When I met with the MD, she explained clearly just how important the service is. There are very strict guidelines to how a customer is received and greeted in store. The system is finely tuned to ensure that the customer knows they have been noticed, but is left to browse by the staff member who remains on hand if needed.

Service is at the core of the company's success. The White Company artfully managed the communication of value to customers to the extent that it's as trusted as John Lewis.

A customer who has trust is a loyal customer, and a growing business pivots around repeat custom.

So now we know we must communicate clearly, engage and listen. It's no different online. The same standards apply to digital and ecommerce. Your website and interactions with it need to be aligned with what a customer might experience in store.

> '*The hard part is the back-end functionality and continual data analysis now. If the user experience is not seamless, then it's pointless, because it is really hard to get people to come back to your website if their first experience is disappointing. Getting the logistics, the processes, the structure and the payment function seamless is vital in order for you to understand the behaviours of your customer and gather useful data.*'
> Paula Reed, Fashion and Brand Consultant

US-based ecommerce platform The RealReal made headlines recently in the *Financial Times*. It resells pre-used designer items, much like you would on eBay. However, the business is positioned cleverly, making its user interface high-end and incredibly user-friendly. Although The RealReal cites its USP as making sure customers have an upbeat, upmarket experience, owner Julie Wainwright says in the FT interview, '*We have a deep appreciation of the brands, the products, the quality and craftsmanship.*' Other key words she used in the interview were 'trust', 'integrity', 'curation' and 'sharing'.[7]

Julie's business is an elegant solution to customers having little space to store unwanted and almost new designer clothes. Now valued at $200million, her premiere luxury consignment company is a runaway success. The true innovation is the service it delivers, making the experience of selling unwanted fashion a delight rather than a drag.

Whilst working with ME+EM I noticed that Clare was constantly examining whether she could improve the website checkout process. She was advised that removing one step might make things more streamlined. On taking the decision to take one security measure out of the process, the brand saw completed transactions jump by 20%.

Whilst that was a great result, the journey to becoming an established ecommerce brand, Clare says she's learnt many other lessons.

> 'To be a trusted E Commerce fashion business means being absolutely watertight on security, protecting customer data and keeping you're the security upgrades constantly up to date. You've seen it. Big companies completely messed up. It goes back to customer trust. You have to make them feel that they can trust you with their data.'
>
> Clare Hornby, Creative Director and Founder, ME+EM

Is your site asking customers to make unnecessary steps? Can you make it easier for them to give you their money? Making the journey smooth for customers is what everyone needs to look to address. How can it be better, faster, easier? Getting that right can be part of your USP and build customer confidence.

Returning to James, what did he learn from his customers? Over three months, the feedback was phenomenal as the customers were so surprised by the engagement. James discovered there were three main issues with the product that he would never have known if he'd not asked customers.

The top three issues he uncovered:

- Colour and dyes, when washed, become naturally faded, which concerned some customers
- Fit was too contemporary for many customers who ordered a few sizes to try them on
- Natural twist and slubs in the jersey yarn were misinterpreted as faults

On the whole, the proportion of customers who had these issues was quite small, but James is so driven to make sure his customers are happy, he was keen to eradicate the issues.

- Colour and dyes – James revised the product stories, making it clear that the natural fading is intended and part of the charm and character of the garment.
- Fit too contemporary – he revised the fit spec on the website to make it much clearer which size to buy
- Natural twist and slubs in the jersey yarn – he created a special film about the fabric's manufacture, showing the process and making it clear the fabric's natural look was highlighted as a benefit, not a fault.

From this exercise, James gained valuable stories from clients – some telling him of how his simple Ts had saved them hours of packing time when they went on holiday as they are such great quality, but also very practical. Others talked about the trips they had been on.

James made a decision to dedicate part of his website purely to packing tips from clients, where they can share their adventures and photos. He called it the 'T Zone' and encouraged them to engage and share. Activity grew on the

T Zone, and within a few months, many customers were jumping in and communicating.

James now has clients who are totally engaged and connected with his brand. He has made them feel like a valued part of a community and has gained their trust. And guess what – they will be buying from him again.

What about James's relationship with his wholesalers? He may well just have a collection of T-shirts, but for his wholesale meetings, he is well prepared. He supplies the store with not only the line sheet of the season, but also a lovely presentation including pictures of his first trip to Japan, visiting his girlfriend's dad's textile business.

He talks about the journey so far, what makes it personal to him, and shows all the inspirations behind the brand identity. He has creative clarity and can talk for hours about the fabrics, his colours, and why it took fifteen attempts to get the perfect blue colour he now calls Duke Blue. He gives them a whole brochure with his brand values, and his key words.

The wholesalers are totally entranced by James and take the brand on board. James is adamant he wants to come to brief the stores when the stock comes in so he can explain his story in person. He has a whole written piece that he's keen for the staff to use when they're talking about the product details, the quality of the fabric, how it's unique and the colours.

The wholesalers smile and agree, knowing the brand will fly. James has given them a rich toolkit through which they can communicate value right through to the end customer.

Many fashion brands fail to understand that this extra little piece of work can produce so many benefits. When the sales staff are excited about the brand, how much more will they sell? Remember that your rate of sell-through is the deal breaker when wholesalers decide whether to buy again the next season.

QUICK EXERCISES

- Who is your target customer and why?
- Which channels would you need to reach that customer?
- How do you keep your customers engaged?
- How do you seek customer insights and feedback?
- Name three reasons why they would recommend your brand?

The key to customer loyalty today is to understand them implicitly, solve an issue for them, then solve another and another. Getting them to engage means they invest in a relationship with your brand. Do that and they will keep coming back for more.

Benefits:

- It makes you an authority on your target client
- It clarifies the one thing you deliver to them
- It makes you strategic about marketing
- It enables you how to engage and retain your customers
- It builds trust, community and brand fans over the long-term

Outcome:

All that detail and time spent getting your product to be the best it can be, backed up by a clear message means you are able to deliver your brand promise. With a strategic and inclusive approach to communications with customers, by engaging for the long-term you will create an army of brand fans, which builds that market trust and gets people talking.

CHAPTER 7

Numbers

'James, we can break you in the UAE,' says a persuasive wholesale agent.

It's tempting. The agent promises that he can expand James's brand into international territories and that the market in the UAE is the one to watch.

James has already secured wholesale accounts in key concept stores – L'Eclaireur in Paris, Corso Como 10 in Milan and Dover Street Market. Granted, he had to supply the stock on sale or return for the first season, but his product was a hit and he now has a waiting list.

Could the same happen in the UAE? James doesn't know enough about the market there. Are there concept stores like the ones in Europe? Would the shoppers there 'get' his brand?

Clearly, he needs to do some homework.

At this point, James owns 80% of the company, with the remainder owned by his fiancée's father, who invested at the start. He wants to grow his business so he can keep control of the creative side and maintain the integrity of the core values. He does not want to become a huge corporate company, but sees potential to grow to around £10 million within six years. He has not thought about the exit strategy yet, but would consider selling.

This is the point in the lifetime of his business where James needs to think about the medium to longer term. He can't make guesses or jump into situations blindly, and neither can you. You need data. And data = numbers.

Product consistency builds trust. By consistency, we're talking about aligning consistency of the fit, fabric quality, design integrity and price. We then have to add a fifth element to make the others work in a commercial way.

If you want your business to grow sustainably, you have to be familiar with all the elements of your company, and that includes the numbers. Sound financial planning enables you to deliver your brand promise, your great and improved product with consistency. It is challenging, but it doesn't have to be a chore. You can get your accounts to reflect more fact than fiction. Get your books in order and you are then free to think creatively and move forward rather than fighting fires.

I've left the numbers part of the ALIGN sequence till last for a reason.

As with any form of data, your accounts and finance reflect only the assumptions that you input. You may have heard of 'rubbish in: rubbish out' (or the cruder version). If you don't have a clear plan for your company, then your finance people will most likely be making decisions based on inaccurate information. Soon, the numbers will influence where the business goes rather than vice versa. And if those numbers are based on 'rubbish'...

To run a fashion business successfully, you have to find some way to be objective about it. You can't let your passion and optimism blind you. For established companies, with dedicated finance roles and departments, it should be easier to find this objectivity. Yet in my experience, there can be a real disconnect between the creative and financial sides of the business, especially in larger firms. In many cases, you'd be hard pushed to detect they had the same goals at all with each happy to work in their own universe, unaligned.

Communications between both sides have to be open and transparent with willingness, creativity, and problem-solving attitudes that carry the business forward. Independent businesses may even have an advantage here. Many are quite simply too small not to be aligned. There is not yet a clear division between the creative and the financial.

As business gets tougher, even established and luxury companies are looking for answers and wondering whether they can learn something from the agile new niche business that are making great strides. They are seeing the need for more entrepreneurial thinking and a less corporate approach.

The owners of independent brands tend to be either owner/designers, who come from a fashion background and typically leave the finance and business planning to others, or owner/entrepreneurs, who look at the opportunity first. Most likely the latter will have great business skills, but often they don't know how to make exceptional product. Both types make incorrect assumptions, which lead to ineffective business plans.

Recognise anyone?

During my research, I asked my influencers what skills are needed today to run a successful fashion brand. Of course, they said the key words like talent, drive and passion. More telling was that they responded without hesitation:

- A head for numbers
- An understanding of the business
- An understanding of the production process

In other words, if you want to run a successful fashion business, you have to understand the numbers.

Enthusiastic designers launch their own brands because they believe, as I once did, that their business will be a platform to express their vision over a lifelong career. Many ignore the inconvenient truth that a fashion business that lasts must get the numbers and finance straight. Depressingly, 90% of new fashion businesses tend to go under in between two and five years, and the lost investment can be anywhere between hundreds of thousands and millions of pounds. Let's not even think about the time and energy wasted.

Fashion is a long-term investment (investment is really what it is). It is very labour and cash intensive. Without a plan, you'll always be working reactively and constantly surprised and bewildered by issues that crop up. You don't want to be a firefighter.

Leaving out planning and financials is a common and avoidable mistake. It may astonish you to learn that companies go bust with full order books purely because they could not raise finance at the right time to produce. You can't predict every eventuality, but you can plan to avoid predictable cash flow problems.

'*You've got all the quality issues ironed out so you need to make sure you can deliver. Make sure your logistics are in place to actually get product to store on time. If not, the big guys are going to be unforgiving for many seasons until you're ready to get back in there again. You absolutely need to have the framework in place before even knocking on the door of one of those big retailers.*'

Barry Woods, Managing Director, Life Fashion Recruitment

Creative accounting

Creativity needs to be applied to finance with as much passion as it is applied to design. Through the ALIGN method, you will form your new assumptions for the business in the short and longer term. These new assumptions will impact on your finance. Managing this change takes a clear head, courage and confidence, but also creative resourcefulness. Do this correctly and you will gain control of your business.

I'm filled with dread when I ask business owners about turnover and margin and hear a reply such as, 'I've no idea! I leave the numbers to my spouse. I'm just the creative.' It's worse when the spouse does not come from a fashion background and has no experience in the sector.

I understand the reluctance to take ownership of this area. Many designers feel that finance, admin and data entry are counterintuitive, but discomfort is rather better than closing the door for ever.

'*It doesn't come naturally to designers to do paperwork. IT and finance is the opposite of what they want to do. They want to do hands-on work, not typing. They can do it quickly, but data entry is boring for them. If they don't understand the profit and loss and balance sheets – I don't have much hope for them unless their partner supports them. Someone in the business has to understand these factors.'*

Marcia Ann Lazar, Founder and Managing Director, Zedonk

You as a business owner must understand every element of your brand and the running of your company. Take responsibility for it now.

Let's look at the four areas of your 'house' that you can simplify to ensure you have the finance and structure to deliver your new and authentic brand. This chapter is split into four sections as it's a big topic. They are called the Four 'S's and are the pillars of your fashion business. The stronger you make these, the more time you will have to drive your business forward:

- Strategy – business planning and growth
- Structure of the business team
- Systems – internal and external organisation
- Security of finance – planning for costs now and in the future

Niche Product
Range Plan
Distribution Strategy
Price Architecture
Key Business Goals

Team Structure
Team Ability
Work Flow
Expertise Requirement

STRATEGY

STRUCTURE

N

SECURITY

SYSTEMS

Business Planning
Manage Cash Flow
Current/Future Finance
Contingency Plans

Critical Path
Design
Production
Logistics
CRM/Data

Part One – Strategy

- Key business goals
- Range plan
- Distribution strategy/partners
- Price architecture

'*You need to be strategic even as a tiny brand. You have to have the time to breathe, which means you need to have enough financial resources, because you can't always compromise. Without financial support, it is impossible to make it. See how innovations such as the electric car were not built on a flimsy budget. You can be as strategic as your finances, but it is important to know what you want.*'

Andrea Ciccoli, Co-founder of The Level Group

Key business goals. Knowing what kind of business you want to run is incredibly important as it will save time and energy. Is it a lifestyle business in which you will be owner, founder and creative for ever? Perhaps it's a business you want to grow to a global brand and sell on later. Where do you want to be in two years' time? Five years' time? How will you know if you're on target? What are your indicators?

It's a competitive market so use your resources wisely. Being focused on what you want the business to look like in a few years helps you work out what you need to implement now. Think of it as 'reverse engineering the future'.

Remember that growing into a brand means most likely raising capital by selling equity. Many businesses look for investors as a way to inject the know-how and funds needed to build the brand quickly. You will attract quality investors only if you can produce a convincing investor 'deck' with detailed finances showing growth. However, gaining investors means relinquishing full control of running your company. Suddenly you are accountable to others and beholden to meet growth targets.

> '*If you want to create a brand, that is a very different experience and journey compared to lifestyle fashion businesses. You have to see growth and improvement on margin every year. If you choose to be a lifestyle business, your sales can stop at any time, but if you are a brand you give yourself the extra task of growth.*'
> Adam Brown, Founder and Creative Director, Orlebar Brown

You may prefer to be your own boss. Funding your own business means you retain control, but you may grow less quickly. The choice is yours. Whichever form of funding you choose, though, will impact all the decisions you make.

Range plan. Customers are no longer buying total looks. Fashion is turning to style and modular dressing. The ratios of how many tops to bottoms you'll need to have in your range is not so predicable any-more. Ranges will be built around what the customers are looking for and what's right for you. It's a fact that many retailers are not reacting to quickly enough.

So for big companies, the task will be to consolidate their offer, while smaller brands moving into their space look to expand without losing their identity. Both large and small companies face the same dilemma: with so much uncertainty, how do they evolve their range without diluting their message? This where the real skill lies.

Extending (or reducing) your range needs to be done with

great care and attention. It's a case of testing and measuring the response, setting timelines and budgets then deciding if you will pursue or not. It's essential that everything you extend into contains part of your brand DNA.

Adam from Orlebar Brown had a recent dilemma. Not long ago, he launched a women's collection.

> '*It was a great success. In fact, the most profitable part of the collection that season, and yet, when we did the numbers we realised that the added staff and resources to deliver that range just weren't worth it.*'
> Adam Brown, Founder and Creative Director, Orlebar Brown

Distribution strategy/partners. Partnering up with like-minded stores is a slower but more controlled way to grow a business, and is one that will provide you with longer-term clients and put you in front of the right type of customers.

If you have, for example, a highly intellectual or sculptural day collection, then align with a store such as Dover Street Market or Corso Como. If a smaller boutique, perhaps outside London, approached you and it was well curated and located in a great area of town, you might consider this account too. However, if you take orders from any shop without understanding what it stands for, you are unlikely to sell. Even if you do sell, you're unlikely to be reaching the right customers who will buy again. Also, if your target customer finds an inconsistent mix of stores distributing you, what message does that send? Don't make decisions that devalue and dilute your message.

When you choose how and where you'll stock, go back to your touch points, your brand guidelines. Either do the research yourself or ask for advice. Think hard whether each store is the right type of store for you.

CASE STUDY – YULAN

Over the few years that I ran my own collection, I made the terrible mistake of jumping from one showroom to another. This happens if you are unclear of your direction. If I had done my research, I would have identified and interviewed the various showrooms before I started selling. Instead, I just picked the best.

I started back to front, with representation at one of Milan's biggest and best-known showrooms, named Studio Zeta. The most important buyers in the world saw my collection that season and they loved it. The problem was that it was effectively a pilot sample collection and not ready for sale.

Although I had interested manufacturers in the pipeline, I should never have pushed the button before everything was aligned. Jumping before I was ready meant a catalogue of problems. Subsequently, I moved to four different showrooms in total.

I had no strategy. As you can imagine, the buyers were confused and got the impression of inconsistency. That word alone is enough to scare any buyer. I struggled season after season to convince buyers that despite a shaky start, that I was a serious brand and could deliver, but it was too late.

As the saying goes: 'You only have one chance to make a first impression.' Lesson learned.

Price architecture

'The most important thing is margin. You have to set your business knowing clearly what your exit margin is. The moment it falls below that, it won't be profitable. Creating

that strategy that means you've got to understand what your intake margin is in relation to that. You also have to understand your discounting model and everything else too. And that is one hell of a piece of maths. To get it right you need a very clever merchandiser who works really well with your finance person. The maths of the business and the creativity has to be completely aligned.'

Clare Hornby, Creative Director and Founder, ME+EM

' We all hate margin, but if you ignore it, you'll eat cash and make no money. You might have lovely jumpers, but there's no point if you don't make any money and stop growing. Whether you are an omni channel, wholesale model or a direct model – all aspects from pricing and margin to sourcing are important.'

Adam Brown, Founder and Creative Director, Orlebar Brown

' Businesses generally believe that they know their gross profit margin, when in fact most of the time, due to a lack of understanding, their figures do not add up. In some cases, businesses are even making gross losses, which means that they are selling their products/garments for less than what they cost to produce.'

Panayiota Viglas, Nordens Accountancy

CASE STUDY

A few years ago, I worked with an established brand on developing their ready to wear collection. It was a perfect fit for me, with my high-end Italian luxury background and this UK based company producing most of their collection of tailoring in Italy.

After working together for a short period, the MD asked me to help with the strategy of a soon to be launched luxury collection, including the price architecture and positioning.

The brief was duly handed over to the newly hired Creative Director of the luxury collection.

Things started going awry when I saw the expensive fabrics that were being chosen, the gorgeous bespoke metalwork being developed, and intricate sketches coming through. This was luxury for sure, but extravagant designer-level development, much like Armani's first line Borgonuovo collection. The samples coming back were beautiful: wasp-waisted couture-like jackets in cashmere, lined with layers of silk, grosgrain and padding. There were dresses in silk zibeline with origami pleats; hand-fringed pockets on complex coats in shimmering couture jacquard silks. They were stunning.

The problem was, no one knew how much they would cost to make, never mind potentially sell for. As the creative journey continued, culminating in a catwalk show during Milan Fashion Week, it seemed that any concept of line plan or pricing strategy had been thrown out the window.

Right up to the last moment, as the clothes arrived in the sales show room in Milan, no one was in possession of a definitive price list. Just as buyers began to arrive, so too did the costings. It became apparent as the list was finalised that the collection would be impossible to sell at a reasonable price without making a loss. Intrinsically the designs were far too complex, making them very labour intensive, and all the materials were expensive.

After all the hours of creativity and the money that had been poured into its development, the luxury collection was completely unsellable.

Even established brands still make these mistakes. The above example makes a great case for the importance of research and being aware of where you are positioning your brand. Be clear the product you deliver is competitively and appropriately priced, and that you can bring your unique vision to market at the level of quality and in your preferred fabrics and still make the margin.

Part Two – Structure

- Team structure
- Team ability
- Workflow
- Expertise requirement

Team structure. Does the structure of your company work? Can it in its current form deliver your new strategy? Whether you have a team of 5 people or 500 or 5,000, looking at this part of the business with clarity is quite terrifying. With big corporate companies, of course, it's a strong CEO who's hired to make these changes.

Ralph Lauren, for example, is going through a huge change in structure. It's a move that became necessary due to over-expansion and brand dilution. In 2015 they hired a new CEO called Stephan Larsson, whose background is H&M and Old Navy. It was a radical appointment as his background was considered a misalignment with a luxury brand like Ralph Lauren, but what the company needed was a fresh perspective.

> ' ...*another culprit was the bloated management structure, he said, which is one reason he is reducing the number of layers between entry-level employees and himself to six, from nine. The reductions will return the executive ranks to roughly 2012 levels.*'
>
> Financial Times, reporting on the reasons for the sweeping changes at Ralph Lauren

By early 2017, his sweeping ideas had hit rough terrain, ending up in disputes with the board and he left. This is telling example of how the revolving door of fashion keeps turning as brands struggle to find a clear forward strategy and balance the experience of brand online and off.

If you are running your own brand in a particular way, it's best practice to revisit the team and structure to make sure they're taking you in the right direction. Couture houses, designer brands, buying-led retailers, high street and ecommerce businesses all have different structures. When I explain this during my lectures to fashion students, they are amazed at how differently companies work and where creative sits in that structure, and that's because it never seems to be taught. This is the reason why it's important to know what kind of business you want to have. Choose it clearly as it will dictate the team and structure you create.

The digital revolution is also making a big change in companies. You will find that CEOs of future fashion will be from a tech-savvy background and digitally aware.

'*Many of them have already undertaken significant cost-cutting and restructuring exercises, and are now primed to capture the benefits.*'[1]

BoF/McKinsey, *The State of Fashion Report 2017*

H&M is a great ecommerce and retail giant. It is constantly innovating and finding new ways to excite the customers, and has been at the forefront of collaborating with top designers and listening to customers' needs. H&M's strength is its approach to diversity. It remains ahead of the curve and relevant, the first of the high street chains to have understood the seismic shift in consumer behaviour. It will be closing stores to invest in online and digital presence. This means a company restructure.

In the more forward-facing companies which are embracing digital, there's a real step change and diversion of funds, both in the marketing team and marketing budgets. While the design processes and development might be carrying on as usual, whole offices have appeared of new staff who are plugged into ecommerce, sales, statistics, analytics, data and keeping on top of online content and social media.

However, no one at this time knows for certain what the return on investment will be. We're still in uncharted territory, and things are moving ahead fast.

Here's where the big opportunity lies. From huge million-dollar corporates to small independents, everyone is talking about how to handle the investment in digital strategy.

Smaller brands have an edge now, being more compact and agile. So yes, although your budget might not extend to that of more established companies, if you ALIGN your business and think creatively, you have a good chance to be seen and heard.

> ‘ *Big brands do find it hard to get their head around digital strategy. Even seasoned professionals get overwhelmed by the speed of it all. Team meetings are very involving, and digital is impacting all aspects of the business. And the coolest operators have panic behind their eyes. It's a big culture shift and many very smart people struggle to see how they can bend their daily work load to adapt.*
>
> *However small companies often have an advantage in that they are more flexible and can move more quickly. On the other hand, the investment that digital requires to scale is often beyond their reach. You have to be very creative to work*

out how you manage that. I find that many young brands are so accustomed to the role of technology in their lives that they adapt quickly and naturally.'

Paula Reed, Fashion and Brand Consultant

' They might find it easier to keep ahead of the trend before it has even happened. They tend to have more understanding of marketing and the voice of the general public, which helps to build good communication and structure across platforms.'

Lee Lapthorne. Creative Director and Founder, On|Off

Team ability

'Can you find good staff that will stay with you for the next ten years? Your own army of interns sounds attractive but they won't be there for you in the future. You need people who have skillsets that you don't to help you grow.'

Marzia Ann Lazar, Founder and Managing Director, Zedonk

'A lot of businesses fail just because they employ their friends rather than bringing on people who can make a difference and help. Whatever entrepreneurial minds you have, you need to surround yourself with people who genuinely understand what they are doing, whether it's at junior, middle or senior level.'

Mathew Dixon, Global Managing Director,
Karen Harvey Consulting Group

Why is it important to know this now? You need to understand the resources and talent your company must have to be able to deliver. The number and type of staff you employ also depends on the market you are working in and the growth you expect. If you already have a compact team but are looking to grow, how you do so means understanding the processes to make sure you are an effective leader and driver of your business.

> ' *You need to do everything yourself and be involved to understand the business inside out. Once you've got through that phase, it's important to understand and acknowledge your own strengths and weaknesses. For example, you won't hold my attention for more than 30 seconds if you start talking about warehousing or algorithms behind a website – I can't contribute. However, surrounding myself with four or five key people who can do that – that's invaluable. If you ignore any parts of a business such as merchandising, finances, if you are missing a sales director, designer – that unsteadies the business. Don't think you can do everything, because you can't.*'
>
> Adam Brown, Founder and Creative Director, Orlebar Brown

Attracting talent and keeping it requires a fresh approach to business and comes back to who you are and the kind of brand culture you nurture.

Workflow. Whether you approach the structure of your business as design-led or buying-led, whether it's a lifestyle business or an international brand, seek to create clear accountability, responsibilities and workflow practices. You decide what kind of boss you will be.

In big companies, the CEO and HR and management teams have a clear structure, and it's very useful in clarifying roles, responsibility and reporting. Even when you're small and growing, it's possible to create a clear organisation chart. Think about where you sit and what is expected within each role. It soon becomes apparent if the talent exists in your team, and whether the team's 'toolkit' will take you where you need to be.

Fashion is a complicated business. Consistent product comes through detailed and structured workflow. If your team members are inexperienced or have never worked in big companies before, it's unlikely that they will have an efficient design process in place. Your team and workflow need to be in line with how you want the company to run. If you are frustrated, then make changes, take action.

My background is in the luxury business, but I've worked in many different structures from huge corporates to start-ups. I've sometimes been surprised at the inefficiency in companies that have already been trading for years. Designer-led or entrepreneur-led businesses tend to muddle along, learning how to work on the job. They assimilate various work practices and information as new staff arrive and join the team.

Say, for example, a designer joins your team who has worked on the high street and is used to working with buyers. They would operate very differently from a designer who has just come from a brand such as Max Mara. They may have the same number of years of experience in design, but they have completely different backgrounds. If they integrate their practice into your business and change workflow process, confusion will arise.

Take another example: a new garment tech joins your company. They have a certain way of working: measuring, then filing the designs and tech packs on their system. If they change (and improve, perhaps) your system but the rest of the business does not know about these changes, then there's trouble ahead.

If everyone who joins shifts systems, even just a little, then the workflow will become haphazard and tasks might well fall between the cracks. Being clear, getting systems into place will reinforce everyone's responsibility. Make concrete what they are required to do.

From running my business, I know that having my own label was not the experience that I thought it would be. I spent too much time worrying about cash flow and production, and undoing problems caused by bad work practice and unclear workflow. It was a completely different experience to working within a structure. Fire-fighting problems ate into my time to be creative and push the business forward.

Expertise requirement. The business is moving at such a pace that the phrase 'time is money' really does resonate. Whether you are consolidating or looking to grow, it's insider knowledge that gets you answers quickest.

If you value your business then invest in the know-how you need. Get a mentor, recruit expertise, find someone who has done this before and has the missing piece of your puzzle. Acknowledgement of your skills and weaknesses is essential. It's unfortunate that you don't know what you don't know till it's too late.

> *'If you want to succeed in fashion, if you have the drive and skills but need help to grow then enlist the help of a true industry insider with both creative and business acumen (basically enlist Joanne Yulan Jong).'*
> Lucie Muir, Luxury Fashion Journalist

> *'If a brand grows bigger and they have people who are no real experts or partners in the team, then the manufacturers get confused and decide to not work with them if it's too messy and difficult.'*
> Kate Hills, Founder of Make It British

Part Three - Systems

- Critical path
- Design
- Production
- Logistics
- Customer relations management

Many fashion business owners are overwhelmed with the amount of issues and 'dull, uncreative' admin work that they must deal with. I can't tell you that there is a magic wand that makes the development and production process perfect, your clients pay on time and gets rid of all the random chaos. But if you have systems in place, much of this stuff becomes far less problematic.

Disorganisation costs your business money. I was recently approached by a company wanting to expand its trouser collection. It had just five styles of trousers, but even then, the assistant I was working with was confused which was which.

On our first meeting, we discovered that the company's suppliers would change the name of the style when they sent the sample back, e.g. they changed a style called 'Trina' into 'Tracy'. There was no apparent reason for this, but it caused confusion and half a day of picking through emails to work out what was going on.

To grow your business, you need to be organised and efficient with suppliers. Keep one person in charge of communicating with them. Make appointments well ahead of time and stick to them. In the early stage, you may get messed around, especially by big manufacturers who don't value your business (yet), but if you make sure you act professionally, then no fault lies with you.

Luckily for all of us, there is constant innovation in software to help us with the above. And luckily for us designers, there isn't yet an algorithm to design or fit fashion, but there is huge progress in the programs to ease the pain of production. Zedonk is one such piece of software and Marcia is the brains behind it.

'When I had my own brand and began to wholesale, we were thrilled. Buyers loved it and our collection was a great success from day one. However, when we received all the orders, my partner and I started going through the logistics, and processing the orders was a complete nightmare. In those days, we didn't even have computers – everything was processed and calculated manually.

'I was wondering how on earth to organise all the information. I wanted to see it all in one place, not scattered around. We ended up writing all the information on a huge roll of plain wallpaper, and we whizzed up and down a cutting table on swivel seats, methodically writing everything down and collating the information. Just to process the orders took us six weeks.'

Marcia Ann Lazar, Founder and Managing Director, Zedonk

Fast forward fifteen years and Marcia and partner own a fantastic software business that has taken years to refine. How do systems – how does *your* system affect the companies you work with?

'It helps them to grow because they are organised. These days, businesses build their products through systems. For example, through the selling campaign, the fabric buyer can

*go to the sales team and say, "This fabric, stop selling it, I'm
not able to get any more of it." You're getting important data
immediately.'*

Marcia Ann Lazar, Founder and Managing Director, Zedonk

This is a great example of someone who understands the
value of systems. Marcia agrees that if you run a professional
business, have systems and are organised, then in turn you
will attract better staff, partners, suppliers and manufacturers
and be prepared for future funding.

Making the time to create systems means you gain more
time to concentrate on research development and innovation
and design. Concentrate on the work that will keep your
business moving forward.

Critical path. Design teams in big companies are briefed by
financial, production and merchandising departments so
they are clear on the expected breakdown of the collection
(line plan) and how it will be split out further into categories (range plan), and the critical path. This is a meticulous
map that enables the whole team to work to given timings
that usually start almost a year in advance of the collection
hitting the stores.

In response to the changing market, collections are being
dropped in store and online as smaller capsules rather than
twice seasonally. Production is now having to merge ecommerce sales, wholesale, and own brand retail sales. The added
pressure of selling direct from the catwalk plays havoc with
critical path planning, which is more reason to bring it under
tight control.

Although digital is moving fast, the supply chain will take
some time to catch up. For most companies, the critical path

will remain the same. The path is largely governed by the time it takes to produce the garments, and more importantly the time it takes to produce the raw components.

Someone in your business always needs to be in control of this. Keep to the drop-dead deadlines, e.g. design handover dates to suppliers or pattern cutters who will continue the development process. Missing deadlines, any deadlines, and wandering from the critical path has a knock-on effect for you, your stress levels, your team and your business. Agree it at the start of the season and adhere to it.

Design. For many fashion businesses, design is the part of the business that seems to be going rather well as it's viewed as the creative, fun part, so at times it does not come under the same scrutiny as the rest of the business. Yet, this is the fundamental core of what your business delivers.

I've seen many a business where the design has been set up by inexperienced staff, becoming ingrained and 'just the way we do it'. Inefficiency here magnifies problems down through the business, so it's crucial to know firstly what kind of business structure you need and then align that with your design process.

Lack of time management can mean everything is rushed. Sketches are unclear, annotations are misleading, too much input comes from too many people (everyone wants to be a designer), coding systems are erratic and inconsistent, prototypes, samples and lap dips get lost…the list goes on. Each season this costs you hours and margin. For SME brands, it can happen because they have never had the discipline or exposure to best practice of the luxury and high-end businesses.

I've learned that design has to be managed, and only clever management of the critical path allows owners to get back to being creative.

Production.

> *'In my view product always comes first. You just have to give a good product, at a fair price, at the right time. Fashion is creative, but there are specifics, delivery windows, price points and quality.'*
> Maria Lemos, Founder and Director, Rainbowwave

> *'I don't think people are interested in a story that is not supported by a great product – it needs to be authentic and distinctive.'*
> Andrea Ciccoli, Co-founder of The Level Group

Brand message needs to be delivered though exceptional, consistent product. The key is aligning your 'toolkit', i.e. the manufacturing capability, with what you want to deliver as a product. If the manufacturing toolkit that you are using is not in line with your product, you will always be fighting an uphill battle.

> *'Finding the right suppliers and keeping them is probably the most critical part of the business. Only when that piece is unlocked, can the rest of it fall into place. When you're small, you have to go and meet every supplier to show them the brand vision and get them excited. Then you need to nurture that relationship. Send them press clippings, photographs, look books. Send them everything so they begin to feel part of your journey.'*
> Clare Hornby, Creative Director and Founder, ME+EM

The temptation to constantly change suppliers in the hope of getting better prices looks desperate and projects an untrustworthy image. Finding the right suppliers who understand what you want to achieve, who get your brand, is much like finding a photographer who gets your vision. It's about the right fit and building long-term relationships/ partnerships.

> *'Brands who think they can approach any factory with a bad attitude won't get far. You are wrong if you think manufacturers don't know each other or speak to each other. The lack of soft skills can leave you with no factories. My advice is to partner and stick with the factories, build a relationship, but don't put all your eggs in one basket. If a factory knows they will be making 2,000 garments for you, and you'll pay on time, they will have more trust in you and are more likely to give you a better price the following season.'*
> Kate Hills, Founder of Make It British

Getting the production process right is a never-ending task. But here are three key areas you need to align around your product, regardless of your market. They are the Three Fs:

- Fabric

- Fit

- Finish

Messing up any of these will damage your reputation and hinder growth in your company.

Many brands give mixed messages and keep changing.

> *'We have certainly seen brands that have closed where season to season you had no idea what to expect from them.'*
> Mathew Dixon, Global Managing Director,
> Karen Harvey Consulting Group

You will have defined the Three Fs in the process of deciding what your brand stands for. Once you have identified them, make sure they remain consistent.

Let's return to the brand Angela Scott for a moment. On the website, Angela talks about craftsmanship and proudly displays photographs of the manufacturing process and the people behind her shoes. Remember what we have learned about the importance of transparency? This is something to aim for. Angela Scott is able to work with manufacturers so closely that these businesses are happy to associate themselves with her publicly. They demonstrate that the brand and the manufacturers have mutual trust, and are working to a common cause. This kind of relationship takes time.

Being inconsistent is a common mistake with SME brands. Marcia at Zedonk notes that after a season, you might see completely different products.

> ' You need to get this kind of thing out of your system when you're a student. Once you are running a business, you need to apply some business rules. What is your core? It needs to be there and developed until it's perfect. Even if the fabrics change, the core vision should be consistent and remain.'
>
> Marcia Ann Lazar, Founder and Managing Director, Zedonk

Logistics. Logistics can mean many things referring to the practicality and timing of production and manufacture. It can also mean how production is quality controlled, shipped, labelled and warehoused. The importance of logistics – stock control, pick and pack, management of orders and returns – becomes paramount, as your business grows online.

If you don't have systems, you can't deliver consistently. While finance and strategy can excite me, logistics is a world that I sit back and watch in wonder. When I worked with the big Italian companies like Gruppo Miroglio, Gruppo Marzotto, Gruppo GFT, Gruppo Max Mara, it was incredible to see the sort of infrastructure the Ready to Wear business already had even back then. Now other countries have learned from Italy's example. China, of course, has improved on quality and design. Portugal, Turkey, Romania and Poland, once thought to be backwaters, are running slick operations on a par with Italy's. Look closely at the big brands that are dominating the market, like ZARA and Amazon. In spite of the challenging market, these companies have nailed a slick, efficient, fast process of logistics. As business moves even more online and customers demand better, quicker, more personalised services, it's innovative management of logistics that will keep these brands as market leaders. ZARA is innovating throughout the entire development of styles, from concept to delivery to shop floor, the reaction to sales and action taken.

Having logistics under tight control means you are able to deliver consistently. If your business has grown to the point where you need to outsource it, there are companies that deal with everything. Do your research and forge partnerships with trusted suppliers – likeminded businesses that understand and care about yours. They are crucial to your business as they control the customer-facing part of your brand.

Customer relationship management (CRM) On that note, don't forget to be very clear about customer relationship management and the data gathering resources it can offer you. It has to be a watertight process, as you will be relying on its efficiency to build your brand's reputation.

Is this part of the business aligned with what you want to achieve?

Part Four – Security

- Business planning
- Cash flow management
- Current/future finance
- Raising finance
- Contingency

You can't be creative in a fashion business when you are worried about finance all the time. Managing cash flow and finance is a fundamental issue for all fashion businesses, and is exacerbated by the complexity of all the moving parts of the business. There are so many things to think about all at the same time.

Having said that, there are many amazing new pieces of technology and software available to you now that were not available to me when I had my own brand. No one can plead ignorance about looming production bills or the pile of unpaid invoices.

To be free, to be the most creative you can be, understand all the different parts of the business. Either you or someone on your team must have finance under tight control. Recognise that the usual ports of call for business finance – including your own personal money and funds from friends and relatives – will completely dry up if there is no planning. Once that funding has gone, it's gone.

With your business assumptions in place, your financial strategy should take worry and uncertainty out of running your business. Let's make things simpler by breaking them down. I'm no financial guru, but as a strategic/creative, I talk about finance from the point of view of being thorough, having thought things through.

Business planning. Many brands think about writing business plans only when they need to raise finance. Thing is, by that point the figures might not be anywhere near good enough to attract external investors.

So, there is internal and external business planning. The internal version is the working financial mechanism behind your brand. It's important for you to calculate whether your business is a viable one today, tomorrow and in the long term. If you haven't got this under control, invest in business plan forecasts and cash flow forecasts.

> ' Targets will be set based on business owners' personal goals of where they would want to be in 1, 2, 3, or 5 years, and with regular management accounts, they will be able to match targets with actual figures to see what needs to be done to achieve the end goal. You would not get in a car without knowing your destination, otherwise you will never get there, and it is the same with business. This will also allow issues to be addressed before they become a problem to the business.

> ' Spend the time understanding your business model and setting appropriate gross profit margins to cover your costs and overheads. This will ensure that you are at least making gross profits and not having to keep re-financing the company using your own personal money. This is key to running a successful and sustainable business in the fashion industry.'
>
> Panayiota Viglas, Nordens Accountancy

Fashion is a high-risk business and a long-term investment. Those who are already in business must take this opportunity, streamline their thoughts and process and take ownership of the business finance, ultimately focusing on where the money will be best invested.

The external or investor business plan, otherwise known as an investor deck, is a completely different type of plan to an internal business working document. The great news is that if you follow the ALIGN method, your new reinforced brand, values and language, backed up with solid research and financials, will be exceptional, and you'll already have prepared a great deal of content for your investor deck.

CASE STUDY – YULAN

My Yulan collection was going well, but as with most independent brands, I saw cash flow issues. Sales were inconsistent, so running the business was becoming stressful. I could not put off doing my business plan any longer, and I needed to raise finance.

I found a reputable firm and commissioned it to do a full business plan and financials for me. I was desperate to get the business under control, and some answers to questions. When do I break even? When do I start to make profit? The consultant asked for everything I had so far so she could pull together a picture of the business. I was so relieved.

I was already three years into the business so I dusted off my business plan (yep, it was in a drawer and missing the financials). I had some track record of sales with wonderful stockists such as Matches, Flannels and Net a Porter, along with great press coverage in *Vogue* and the *International Herald Tribune*, so naturally I thought I had a strong case and the ingredients of success.

The consultant helping me took time to go over my assumptions and noted all the sales and costs that I'd racked up to date, then arranged to meet with me a few weeks later. I was excited and nervous and hopeful. Unfortunately, on sitting down with me, she said the figures did not look promising and she had 'bad news'. My collection was high-end, expensive to develop and produce, and directly in competition with established brands that were better known and better financed.

In short, the figures did not stack up.

I think she was taken by surprise when I spontaneously burst into tears and could not stop. I realised that it did not make sense to carry on. It was not a sustainable business. There was a clear disparity between the overheads of the business and the turnover of sales.

This was a simple sum which I could have done years before, but deep down I knew what the result would be. That's why I had avoided it.

I see many brands heading down the same path. It's the reason why I've created the ALIGN method to simplify and clarify the process by which you can address issues fast without breaking down in tears in front of a consultant.

Cash flow management. Changing to cloud-based accounts was a massive game changer as it freed up so much of my time. Most big fashion companies use software such as Xero, Sage or QuickBooks, or even FreeAgent. Knowing what's happening in your business and being able to see that at a glance whenever and wherever you like puts your mind at rest and flags up issues in real time. It doesn't have to be hard to get organised in this way.

'*It is quite worrying how many businesses we come across that do not produce forecasts, and more importantly cash flow forecasts. Cash flow is vital to any business, as without cash being available to run the day-to-day business, the business does not work.*

'*What this means is that a business may get a customer who may put in a big order, but without the cash for manufacture/ production costs, the sale would be lost. Lack of cash flow forecasts would also damage the chance of raising finance in these circumstances. A cash flow forecast allows businesses to pick up these issues before they happen, allowing for growth and flexibility.'*

Panayiota Viglas, Nordens Accountancy

Creative thinking around cash flow is a challenge, but one that doesn't have to be negative. Remember how Everlane successfully challenged the typical business model?

Current/future finance. Consistent delivery all comes down to understanding the process and planning everything meticulously far ahead of the season. And if you're crunching those numbers alongside this, you will gain traction in a crowded market.

What is your current and future route to finance? If you need to raise finance, who will you approach and when?

While a few stellar businesses might be snapped up by the likes of the Kering Group or LVMH, most fashion businesses raise funds through smaller private equity investment and venture capital funding. Alternatively, look at peer-to-peer lending and crowd-funding through platforms such as Kickstarter and Crowdcube. Again, it comes down to what you want to do: give away products or equity, or neither.

You must, as ever, be strategic. Financial planning gives you the means to make choices. Running out of funds is an all-too-common story, and reaching out when you are in a rush means making mistakes, overlooking details and risking signing away part of your brand unnecessarily.

Many designers and fashion companies keen to grow their business quickly will agree to sell much more of it for much less money than they expected. It might be better to take a little more time to strengthen your position before you take that step.

'*Sometimes it just comes down to seeing it through for another season or a couple of seasons to get it more developed and powerful in the market. Likewise, have a very real sense of the value of the brand at an early stage and realise that an investment in the business doesn't always mean rapid growth.*'

Mathew Dixon, Global Managing Director,
Karen Harvey Consulting Group

Raising finance. If an investor has become interested, resist the temptation to agree to sales targets that are clearly not feasible. Making a business plan that is based on fiction not fact is a recipe for stress.

'*If you are giving part of your business to a private equity business or group, that puts tremendous pressure on you as business. It changes the dynamic of the business because you must deliver against pre-agreed times. It's not a magic bullet, but I've seen designers given crazy growth targets. They didn't realise if you don't hit the growth targets, you will lose control of your business and a greater control of equity. There are plenty of people out there whose names are on the top of the door who own a very small part of a brand, but in reality, don't have control of it anymore.*

'*Don't sell your name or your business too soon. One brand who is going for a second round of funding now is really struggling because they gave so much equity away on the first round of funding and now the business is becoming diluted. As a result, they can't raise the capital they want because they don't have the volume of equity left to be able to support that.*'

Mathew Dixon, Global Managing Director,
Karen Harvey Consulting Group

If you already have ideas of who you might partner with or approach for future finance, investigate and 'court' them early. Make sure you take your time to find out about them. It can take years to seal the right deal with the right partner or investor and your aims for the business need to be taken into consideration.

Contingency. With the best will in the world, you can't plan for every eventuality. Sort out your contingency budget. Many brands add a margin onto each product to cover any mishaps such as cancelled orders, production issues, or an unexpectedly high level of customer returns. You never know what the glitch might be and when it will come along.

CASE STUDY – YULAN

When I had my collection, one of my designs was embroidered with trouser hooks in a beautiful gunmetal colour. These were layered on each other so they looked like medieval armour plating. I had numerous test swatches done, and everyone agreed that although it was expensive to produce, it was going to be well worth it. The samples were breath-taking and the buyers loved them, so I took orders that season and they went into production.

Several months later, the box of placed embroideries for production duly arrived at the office. I was out the morning it arrived so my assistant signed it for. When I opened the box that afternoon, I noticed that some of the placements were looking great and others not so. To my dismay, the hooks had turned a strange colour, and on closer inspection I realised they had rusted, although the box was perfectly dry.

I called the embroidery company and spoke to someone there who could not work out what had caused the rust either. We spent a few days deliberating and worked out finally what had happened.

The shipment had come by sea. The shipping container must have leaked during transit and the box had at some point got wet. The box had dried out, but the placements remained damp enough to allow rust on what I'd thought were rustproof trouser hooks.

There was nothing I could do. I didn't have the money or the time to reproduce them ready for delivery to stores. I couldn't ask for compensation as my office had signed for the box, declaring the goods were delivered in satisfactory condition. Who could have predicted that?

The unexpected always happens in fashion production. Cancelling those expensive pieces from the orders meant the delivery became fragmented, the stores were cross and a huge hole was left in my cash flow. Having a contingency in place would have meant I could have minimised damages.

Consistency of delivery is essential for the success of your brand. Your product is only as good as the systems you use to produce it. Crunching the numbers and understanding process means you'll reduce uncertainty and take control of your business. Being clear about your goals and the steps needed to achieve them fosters confidence and motivation for you and your team. Free up your time to concentrate on what you do best.

The continuing story of James and Brand X

James has set his three-year plan goals to grow and test organically while not overstretching himself. He has been approached by a wholesale agent who has promised that he can expand Brand X into international territories, saying that the market in the UAE is doing well and James would be a big success there.

However, James has decided this is not the route for him.

He wants to sit in concept stores only – stores where he knows his brand will be discovered. He's done his research and knows that there are no concept stores in Dubai, plus the body shape of the men there is different to what he has developed. The brands men in Dubai buy are polarised to either designer-level or cheap, so Brand X would be tricky to explain in that market. It's too sophisticated. Although there might be potential sales there, James thanks the agent and says he'd like to keep the opportunity for the future.

James owns 80% of the company with 20% owned by his fiancée's father. He's so passionate to keep control of the creative side and maintain the integrity of the business that he decides in order to position his brand in a bigger market, he will expand his business through collaborations and partnerships.

Through his connections at L'Eclaireur, James is introduced to the owner of a hotel business in Japan looking to commission uniforms for a new cutting-edge series of hotels. The owner is a fan of James's T-shirts, and now James has orders on his books for a new customised T made especially for the hotel chain. As part of the deal, the chain will give him a space in its hotel shops and host an event for him when he launches the new series of product.

James has a huge success with the Ts and is contacted by an investor who wants to help him open a boutique. James can show year on year growth in his business and impresses the investor with the brand journey so far. Although James wanted ideally to keep a high share of his company, he considers selling 29% to the investor (retaining 51%) in return for this incredible opportunity.

On hearing this news, the father of James's fiancée comes up with a proposal, which is a much better option. He will let James work directly with the factory to experiment, manufacture and develop new fabrics. He will also partially fund a flagship store in Japan giving him a direct route to his customers. His future father-in-law does not have a huge budget, but he is very well connected. James intends to test the retail model first, contacting the investor once he knows it works.

James has a great head on his shoulders and a clear vision. Opportunities arise because his strategy reflects his brand and he is guided by the principles and integrity of what he has created. He knows what type of business he wants to be, how he wants to run it and what he wants out of it.

However, James does make mistakes.

He had developed a whole range of denim, hired a denim specialist and an assistant to help source fabrics specifically for that collection. However, when James decided to concentrate on his Ts and focus on e-commerce, he slowly began to realise that he would have to let the denim team go. With that budget he could get better photography and a digital marketing assistant.

The time he was going to spend developing the denim collection would, he knew, be better-spent visiting target stores and igniting relations with them.

James was at the same time looking at his wholesale strategy. He makes a bold decision not to push wholesale anymore and removes his collection from the showroom that represents him. In his mind, the distribution margin he would save would be better invested in improving the CRM on his website.

With so much going on, James decides to postpone closing the denim division for six months. This decision alone will see him wasting tens of thousands of pounds in overheads. Even worse, James gradually reduces the workload of the denim collection team without an explanation.

With this strange lack of communication the denim

designer starts to get anxious and asks what's happening. The designer has risked his reputation, having persuaded key denim manufacturers that the new collection Brand X would be a great new venture and one that deserved backing. James comes clean and tells the designer he is thinking of stopping the denim collection. The designer, fed up with this news, claims the rest of the season's design fees even though he does not have to design anything.

The factory that was developing the denim has now got wind of the situation and refuses to send the first set of prototypes until it has a clear understanding what's happening. Neither the designer nor the factory is keen to speak with James and Brand X again – he has acted unprofessionally.

Taking the time to review the structure of your business and team is crucial if you are to strengthen your business. As a business owner, when you choose a change of direction, the skills of the team you have in place need to be aligned with the new direction. Communication is important. If your identity changes, you must communicate that to the team then tackle any issues as soon as possible.

If James had communicated his new direction to the designer and the factory, both might have been swayed to postpone the project. Sure, there would have been some negotiation regarding what he would have to pay now, but crucially, James would have been seen as acting professionally.

QUICK EXERCISES

- Does your current team have the expertise needed?
- What systems are in place to streamline processes?
- What key goals have you set and what are the indicators?

- What strategy do you have for your range development?
- Describe how your finance team is linked with creative?

The role of creativity has changed. Creative thinking has to be applied not just to product and design, but also throughout each department. Businesses are looking in detail at how to make the business more streamlined and resilient, but it's a delicate balance to do that and retain the soul of a brand.

Benefits:

- It helps you action opportunities to professionalise
- It helps you take bold decisions from a point of knowledge
- It gives you confidence to plan finance with creativity
- It helps you leverage the ability to think and act quickly
- It empowers you to take ownership of a clear forward strategy

Outcome:

Using the mindset and best practice of the market leaders means you are able to harness the great advantage you have of being smaller and more agile at this momentous time of change. By aligning your creative and strategic vision you'll be able to motivate a dedicated team working together to achieve a single clear objective. Backed up by sound financial planning, you will have the confidence to take control and see new opportunities. Gain that credibility, visibility and grow.

Over To You

> *'Consumers have so many choices that fashion companies need to leverage the information they have to segment and then segment again. Emerging brands have been founded on the realisation that there are many untapped consumers for whom today's fashion brands fail to cater.'* [1]
>
> BoF/McKinsey, *The State of Fashion Report 2017*

The BoF/McKinsey report underlines that as the market fragments, gaps and opportunities will open up. The even better news is the fashion business was valued at $2.4 trillion in 2016 and the indications are that it's projected to grow despite the recent challenges.[2]

> *'As the organizers of major international trade shows we are always researching what is effecting the business. Fashion has been very disrupted by digital, but the reports we've been presented by* KPMG *show that despite the market volatility, the fashion market will still be in growth. Reports predict that it will grow steadily till 2025, much of that growth coming*

from consumers spending more on E Commerce, but also the multi-brand boutiques who get the customer experience right, taking the lead when it comes to wholesale.'

Thomas Johann Lorenz, Director Business Development, Premium Group

The bad news is there's evidence that owner-led independents will lose the most market share.

' Those most at risk are small to medium owner-led independent businesses who are not thinking digital and are unable to differentiate themselves with a uniquely curated portfolio, clearly defined target groups and in-store experiences.'

Thomas Johann Lorenz, Director Business Development, Premium Group

We are really still only at the start of the digital journey so it's not too late to take action.

'Digital technology, despite its seeming ubiquity, has only begun to penetrate industries. As it continues its advance, the implications for revenues, profits, and opportunities will be dramatic.' [3]

McKinsey, 'The Case for Digital Reinvention'

I'm passionate about preventing owners from losing businesses they have worked so hard to create because they don't understand the switch has happened. They don't understand the 'new rules of the fashion business' as they are too busy running their business to see that opportunities are there waiting. Other brands that are savvier will overtake them with ease. The result? They will work harder to get ahead and gain back their market share. The thing is, the external forces of digital are conspiring to make their task ever harder.

I hear business owners say, 'All I need is cheaper production'; 'All I need is a better sales agent'; 'All I need is a great digital marketing strategy'; 'All I need is more money'. Of course, the above would help, but none of these in isolation will build a long-lasting stand-out brand today. It's the alignment of the business that will make it exceptional.

I wrote this book for SME fashion businesses that are looking to move up a level to gain credibility, visibility and growth, but all fashion brands, creative businesses and retailers, large and small, are grappling with the enormous changes in the market. Therefore the ALIGN method will appeal to businesses of all sizes as it addresses the wider issues. However, having information is all very well and the learning journey can be fun, but nothing will change if you don't implement it. And there's no time like the present.

Winner takes all

' Most of the industry value is captured by a small percentage of players, with the top 20 percent creating 100 percent of total economic profit. Fashion is essentially a winner-takes-all industry – a handful of companies that make the right decisions and execute flawlessly are the ones that reap the lion's share of the rewards.' [4]
BoF/McKinsey, *The State of Fashion Report 2017*

There is no time to lose. It's now or never. Digital is here to stay, and more and more we will see fashion sales driven online.

Whether you sell online or not, be clear that your brand and the future of communicating it will be. The top 20% will be concentrating even harder on making sure their brand experience online is seamless.

> ' Bold, tightly integrated digital strategies will be the biggest differentiator between companies that win and companies that don't, and the biggest pay-outs will go to those that initiate digital disruptions. Fast-followers with operational excellence and superior organizational health won't be far behind.' [5]
>
> McKinsey, The Case for Digital Reinvention

Okay, I'm not saying this will be easy. It might seem easier to continue the way you're going already, but you risk letting your competitors sail away with the business that should be yours. Getting it right is worth the effort. I mean, what exactly is the downside of a new, professionalised, focused brand and business that's armed with a laser-sharp message and a passion to deliver excellence?

Entrepreneurs who get ahead have a common trait and that's solution finding. I call it creative resourcefulness, and they only spend money if it furthers their focused business model. Letting things drift is not an option. It drains your capital and it's flowing in the wrong direction.

We are truly living in an extraordinary time. Digital has affected everything in our lives and will continue to do so. We are observing in real time how the different generations engage with it, and all businesses, not just fashion, are having to watch, analyse and adjust to the fragmentation of the market.

For fashion, what is clear is that the rulebook has been torn up and a new era has arrived. Fashion businesses that operative on old methods, old systems, and who fail to acknowledge and engage fully with customers through digital will become irrelevant.

Faster fashion, faster everything

This is the new reality. We are becoming accustomed to making initial judgments quickly so it's key to articulate your value in seconds.

> *'When you are in our stage you need to create a strong story around the product. You have to get the story across to the customer in a nanosecond. The story is confusing; I don't think they will engage with the product.'*
> Adam Brown, Founder and Creative Director, Orlebar Brown

Build that convincing, succinct foundation and true story through the ALIGN method, and you will find focus, strength and conviction.

> *'To connect and stand out, especially online, you have to have one brilliant idea. These days, especially on social media, we make judgments so quickly – the message has to be clear, precise and distinct backed up with a precisely engineered offer. That focus cuts through the white noise.'*
> Paula Reed, Fashion and Brand Consultant

The problem lies in your customer's expectations. If you seek to exceed them then deliver consistently, you will succeed.

> *'These days people spend time and engage differently, and there is a revolution in the customer experience and the value they are looking to receive and what they actually get.'*
> Andrea Ciccoli, Co-founder of The Level Group

The truth is that if customers want great product, they have to be ready to wait for it as the supply chain can't react that fast. That's the current dilemma.

The customer's always right

We are back where we were twenty years ago. I remember when I was a kid, my father used to say, 'The customer's always right.' If you received goods that were not fit for purpose, you'd say so and there would be no trouble getting the issue resolved.

As everything, including customer service, became outsourced, we went through years where things turned against the consumer. Suddenly we customers would have to spend hours online or on a phone, hanging on the line in a queue, waiting for an opportunity to rant, only to be told that 'Computer says no'.

With the digital era, customers have chosen to leave many businesses in droves. With so many products, so much choice and the ability to compare price instantly, it's only right perhaps that the tables have turned again and businesses are fighting to retain customers.

What this represents is a wonderful window of opportunity where research, development and creativity suddenly become of utmost importance. But it's a new kind of creativity, one that's more entrepreneurial, connected together with finance and business, and rooted in current events. It's relevant and no longer done in isolation. Hence the word ALIGN. Creative has to align with the other parts of your business to work.

I'm naturally entrepreneurial, and my belief is: 'There is power at the intersection of entrepreneurship and great design'. If the two come together, that's what makes a successful brand.

Your opportunity

You may be asking right now, 'Is it still possible to break through to become a global brand?'

> '*Absolutely it is possible. Brands like Armani, Dolce Gabbana, have been in the business for years, led by very strong business-men and women who surrounded themselves with loyal teams and dedicated partners. They made it their life's work, and I have seen many young designers today who are following in their footsteps to ensure they experience that same staying power within their own businesses.*'
> Marty Wikstrom, Founder, Atelier Fund and Corporate Director

The good news is that there are plenty of opportunities and benefits to being an SME business in the era of digital fashion. Without a doubt, with economic changes and consumer habits so closely linked, the single most import thing you can do for your brand right now is differentiate. Strengthen your unique story, establish integrity and create value, because that's what shines through. It's the opportunity that smaller businesses can really exploit, and do so in spades.

> '*Creativity, community and other big contributors to this storytelling movement didn't used to be this important. This is why big brands are not in the best position to develop that as they are just struggling to cope with digital, which takes a lot of resources and energy.*'
> Andrea Ciccoli, Co-founder of The Level Group

> '*We are a small and nimble business and have the opportunity to do things more quickly. Change direction if we need to, reverse a decision, go add something to our marketing plan.*'
> Adam Brown, Founder and Creative Director, Orlebar Brown

'*Smaller independents have an advantage, because they can be more flexible and quicker to push content out. They are just a bit more nimble.*'
Matt Booker, Founding Director of COUSIN

'*Don't be distracted from your core goals and stay on that journey, be involved in everything, keep it simple, do one thing well and you'll be remembered for that.*'
Adam Brown, Founder and Creative Director, Orlebar Brown

'*Keep collections to a minimum and reinforce the brand message with better-designed pieces. Today, brands really have to focus on the old adage – less is more.*'
Lucie Muir, Luxury Fashion Journalist

'*It's nice to see small growth spurts and companies who do niche things – how fantastic is that?*'
Caroline Issa, Fashion Director and CEO of Tank

'*Of course they have disadvantages regarding scale, but online has helped smaller challenger brands, giving them the opportunity to create something that at a glance can look like a very expensive photo-shoot. Given we are viewing images on a tiny screen it can be hard to tell the difference.*'
Matt Booker, Founding Director of COUSIN

'*I am kind of shocked the newcomers are not brave enough to be more digital. I still hear them saying "I want to be in Vogue" – and I am surprised. You should be the new guy on the block with fresh perspectives. They don't see what they are trying to get into is instead something they should aim to get out of. I think there is an opportunity there, that very few are moving in to capitalize.*'
Andrea Ciccoli, Co-founder of The Level Group

'Embrace the changing world that we live in and don't be afraid to try something new in order to stand tall above the rest. Embrace the technology, social media, but always stay true to your DNA. In large companies, creative voices are being less heard. Many of the big brands are run by management who don't necessarily listen to creatives. I believe in order for a business to grow, the designers need to have a creative environment. Unfortunately, companies taken over by parent companies don't often nurture creativity and focus more on the numbers, which is stifling for those who are in creative positions.'

Lee Lapthorne, Creative Director and Founder, On|Off

'Fashion players will redouble their focus on branding in order to escape the increasing commoditisation trap. To create value, brands need to be different and maintain clear, strong brand values. At the luxury end, this brand strengthening in 2017 will likely entail a reinvestment in creativity: creating unique products that encapsulate their USP.' [6]

BoF/McKinsey, *The State of Fashion Report 2017*

Will digital change the way people think about fashion? As a designer it's a hard pill to swallow, but yes, this book recognises that digital has put customers first, and will challenge the fundamentals of the fashion business and change the criteria for what it takes to get ahead today. It takes a hungry, open mind to succeed in today's market. You also have to be damn good at what you do.

I accept that I'm challenging the way fashion design is taught to students, many of whom have gone on to form independent fashion companies. The result of their education (without any business training) has them still looking to antiquated benchmarks such as being in a certain magazine or catwalk recognition. These are irrelevant references in the future game. To aim for these is missing the point of today's digital opportunities, and will likely mean these businesses are destined to fail.

Indeed, digital is a stark wake-up call to all fashion businesses that have not addressed the fact that the traditional systems are broken. I see so many companies struggling, but they continue down the same path. While we are still in the business of creating fashion, everything around that is changing.

The ALIGN method explains how it's possible to shine in a noisy, crowded environment. It shows the secrets behind the transformation in the brands I've worked with. This method delivers the change of mindset you'll need, which is invaluable for those who are starting out, but is just as powerful for the ambitious business owners who are focusing, consolidating and creating resilience and sustainability in their business. ALIGN gets them back control with a credible plan and makes their business a digital-savvy, forward-thinking, lean, mean fighting machine. Not only that but they will find clarity around what they need to action to make their brand stand out head and shoulders above the others. They will do that authentically because everything they do will be genuinely linked to personal stories and a journey that is unique.

In conversation recently, the man who has done it all, Giorgio Armani, underlined the importance of being bold and creating strong personal brand foundations.

'Something I always tell the young talented people I meet, like those designers I promote each season by giving them the opportunity to present their collections at the Armani/Teatro,

is to take on the world of fashion with commitment and determination. It is essential, too, for them to have a strong personal point of view, and to be brave enough to express this, because it is only this that will mark out their work as being different. I also think it is crucial to explain that they must never forget that in addition to being creative, they must also be pragmatic. And they should be prepared to work hard, of course. There really is no substitute for hard work; success does not come by chance, or through talent alone.'
Giorgio Armani

Ideas are nothing if you don't action them. Change your definition of what being creative means. New thinking does not happen overnight – make the time. Look at your business as a whole – don't lose yourself in one part of it. Be objective about what type of business you want yours to be. Invest in the time to think, plan and strategise your goals

You can't do it all yourself. Acknowledge your strengths and weaknesses. Learn from experts, and take advice. Don't over reach; it's all about steady growth and building loyal customers.

Going the extra mile really shows. Aim to be the best and deliver what you promise.

These are the new rules of fashion.

REFERENCES AND FURTHER READING

Introduction

1. The State of Fashion 2017. (2016). 1st ed. [ebook] London: BoF and McKinsey & Company. Available at: https://www.businessoffashion.com/articles/news-analysis/the-state-of-fashion-2017 [Accessed 8 Jun. 2017].

Chapter 1 – Ten Influencing Factors

1. Heuveldop, N. (2017). Ericsson mobility report. 1st ed. [ebook] Niklas Heuveldop. Available at: https://www.ericsson.com/assets/local/mobility-report/documents/2017/ericsson-mobility-report-june-2017.pdf [Accessed 28 Jul. 2017].

2. The State of Fashion 2017. (2016). 1st ed. [ebook] London: BoF and McKinsey & Company. Available at: https://www.businessoffashion.com/articles/news-analysis/the-state-of-fashion-2017 [Accessed 8 Jun. 2017].

Chapter 2 – The Five Steps Of Alignment

1. HBR's 10 must reads 2016. (2016). Boston, Massachusetts: Harvard Business Review Press.

2. Tooke, G. (2017). Decline deepens for beleaguered fashion market - Global site - Kantar Worldpanel. [online] Kantarworldpanel.com. Available at: https://www.kantarworldpanel.com /global/News/Decline-deepens-for-beleaguered-fashion-market [Accessed 19 Jul. 2017].

Chapter 3 – Authenticity

1. The State of Fashion 2017. (2016). 1st ed. [ebook] London: BoF and McKinsey & Company. Available at: https://www .businessoffashion.com/articles/news-analysis/the-state-of -fashion-2017 [Accessed 8 Jun. 2017].

2. The State of Fashion 2017. (2016). 1st ed. [ebook] London: BoF and McKinsey & Company. Available at: https://www .businessoffashion.com/articles/news-analysis/the-state-of -fashion-2017 [Accessed 8 Jun. 2017].

3. Ellison, J. (2015). Chanel's Roman holiday. [online] Ft.com. Available at: https://www.ft.com/content/d852e008-99ac-11e5 -987b-d6cdef1b205c?mhq5j=e2 [Accessed 19 Jul. 2017].

4. Mower, S. (2016). Chanel Fall 2016 Couture Fashion Show. [online] Vogue. Available at: http://www.vogue.com/fashion -shows/fall-2016-couture/chanel [Accessed 19 Jul. 2017].

5. Mower, S. (2016). Chanel Fall 2016 Couture Fashion Show. [online] Vogue. Available at: http://www.vogue.com/fashion -shows/fall-2016-couture/chanel [Accessed 19 Jul. 2017].

6. The State of Fashion 2017. (2016). 1st ed. [ebook] London: BoF and McKinsey & Company. Available at: https://www .businessoffashion.com/articles/news-analysis/the-state-of -fashion-2017 [Accessed 8 Jun. 2017].

7. The Business of Fashion. (2017). Stella McCartney | #BoF500 | The Business of Fashion. [online] Available at: https://www .businessoffashion.com/community/people/stella-mccartney [Accessed 8 Jun. 2017].

8. Stoppard, L. (2015). The rise of the monobrands. [online] Ft.com. Available at: https://www.ft.com/content/5a9637d2-dea9-11e4 -b9ec-00144feab7de?mhq5j=e2 [Accessed 19 Jul. 2017].

Chapter 4 – Language

1. O'Flaherty, M. (2016). Breton tops, Basquiat and Bowie: celebrating forty years of Agnès b. [online] Available at: https://www .ft.com/content/131b5870-4748-11e6-8d68-72e9211e86ab [Accessed 19 Jul. 2017].

Chapter 5 – Innovation

1. Ellison, J. (2017). Miroslava Duma's new industrial revolution. [online] Ft.com. Available at: https://www.ft.com/content /d20b61ea-3954-11e7-821a-6027b8a20f23?mhq5j=e2 [Accessed 19 Jul. 2017].

2. Worldforumdisrupt.com. (2017). Luca Marini – MogulCon London 2016. [online] Available at: http://www.worldforumdisrupt .com/mogulcon-london-2016/speaker/luca-marini/ [Accessed 19 Jul. 2017].

3. Del Rey, J. (2016). Online Retailer Everlane Wants to Raise New Money at a Valuation North of $250 Million. [online] Recode. Available at: https://www.recode.net/2016/3/7/11586744/online -retailer-everlane-wants-to-raise-new-money-at-a-valuation [Accessed 28 Jul. 2017].

Chapter 6 – Gain Trust

1. Fleming, J. (2014). The Power of Aligning Consumers With Your Brand. [online] Gallup.com. Available at: http://www.gallup.com /businessjournal/173861/power-aligning-consumers-brand.aspx [Accessed 8 Jun. 2017].

2. Fleming, J. (2014). The Power of Aligning Consumers With Your Brand. [online] Gallup.com. Available at: http://www.gallup.com

/businessjournal/173861/power-aligning-consumers-brand.aspx [Accessed 8 Jun. 2017].

3. Want to talk to me? What customers want in exchange for their personal information. (2015). [ebook] London: Royal Mail MarketReach. Available at: http://www.royalmail.com/business /system/files/Royal-Mail-MarketReach-UK-Consumer-Data -Permissions-Report-2015_0_0.pdf [Accessed 31 Jul. 2017].

4. Tech Trends 2016 Innovating in the digital era. (2016). 1st ed. [ebook] Deloitte University Press. Available at: https://www2 .deloitte.com/content/dam/Deloitte/ve/Documents/technology /DUP_TechTrends2016.pdf [Accessed 1 Jun. 2017].

5. Tech Trends 2016 Innovating in the digital era. (2016). 1st ed. [ebook] Deloitte University Press. Available at: https://www2 .deloitte.com/content/dam/Deloitte/ve/Documents/technology /DUP_TechTrends2016.pdf [Accessed 1 Jun. 2017].

6. Fleming, J. (2014). The Power of Aligning Consumers With Your Brand. [online] Gallup.com. Available at: http://www.gallup.com /businessjournal/173861/power-aligning-consumers-brand.aspx [Accessed 8 Jun. 2017].

7. Stoppard, L. (2016). Consignment websites turn designer cast-offs into cash. [online] Ft.com. Available at: https://www .ft.com/content/5a87a330-ffcc-11e5-99cb-83242733f755?mhq5j=e2 [Accessed 19 Jul. 2017].

Chapter 7 – Numbers

1. The State of Fashion 2017. (2016). 1st ed. [ebook] London: BoF and McKinsey & Company. Available at: https://www .businessoffashion.com/articles/news-analysis/the-state-of -fashion-2017 [Accessed 8 Jun. 2017].

Chapter 8 – Over To You

1. The State of Fashion 2017. (2016). 1st ed. [ebook] London: BoF and McKinsey & Company. Available at: https://www

.businessoffashion.com/articles/news-analysis/the-state-of-fashion-2017 [Accessed 8 Jun. 2017].

2. The State of Fashion 2017. (2016). 1st ed. [ebook] London: BoF and McKinsey & Company. Available at: https://www.businessoffashion.com/articles/news-analysis/the-state-of-fashion-2017 [Accessed 8 Jun. 2017].

3. Bughin, J. (2017). The case for digital reinvention. [online] McKinsey & Company. Available at: http://www.mckinsey.com/business-functions/digital-mckinsey/our-insights/the-case-for-digital-reinvention [Accessed 19 Jul. 2017].

4. The State of Fashion 2017. (2016). 1st ed. [ebook] London: BoF and McKinsey & Company. Available at: https://www.businessoffashion.com/articles/news-analysis/the-state-of-fashion-2017 [Accessed 8 Jun. 2017].

5. Bughin, J. (2017). The case for digital reinvention. [online] McKinsey & Company. Available at: http://www.mckinsey.com/business-functions/digital-mckinsey/our-insights/the-case-for-digital-reinvention [Accessed 19 Jul. 2017].

6. The State of Fashion 2017. (2016). 1st ed. [ebook] London: BoF and McKinsey & Company. Available at: https://www.businessoffashion.com/articles/news-analysis/the-state-of-fashion-2017 [Accessed 8 Jun. 2017].

ACKNOWLEDGEMENTS

Thank you to the scores of friends, clients, entrepreneurs, fashion industry experts, and stand out individuals that took time out of their busy schedules to talk with me. You have my gratitude for sharing your insights, stories and opinions that illustrate beautifully the principles behind this book.

Thanks also to those who took time to beta read and review the book and giving such helpful feedback.

Thanks to the Rethink Press team, to Lucy, Joe and the editorial team.

Thanks to my husband and daughter and family for their patience and support, and encouraging me to keep going.

Final thanks must go to my ever-supportive father and to my late mother. She saw my passion very early on and encouraged me to follow the career of my choice. I've been so fortunate to have such liberal, loving parents.

THE ALIGN PROGRAMME

The ALIGN programme is dedicated to owner led creative businesses, to help them implement a change in mindset, streamline and implement best practices, and stand out.

It's designed to help you understand the shifts in the market and provide a unique check and balance system that creates a clearer, more focused strategic business. It encourages you to address areas that need to be improved and push boundaries; to make your products exceptional, highlight and build on the value you already have, and unlock the potential of your brand.

Through this powerful five-step programme, business owners can fast track to the expertise and answers though learning and implementing. They gain clarity by accessing a high-level network of industry insiders.

Bespoke Services

Following the ALIGN Programme, clients can access a full range of creative and business services relating to each of the five stages. These include creative direction, design and development, right though to production, communication, marketing and business strategy.

If you'd like to know more then find us here: www.yulancreative.com

Yulan Creative
19 Eastbourne Terrace, London W2 6LG
Telephone: 02030360585
Email: info@yulancreative.com

Follow us here on social:
Instagram: yulan_creative
Twitter: yulancreative
Facebook: yulancreative

THE AUTHOR

Joanne Yulan Jong is the successful London-based fashion designer, creative director and author. A natural entrepreneur, she started selling her collections to stores aged just fifteen. Her late teens saw her apprenticed to couture houses in London and Paris whilst studying at Edinburgh College of Art and The Royal College of Art.

On graduating, her talent was quickly snapped up by luxury fashion house Giorgio Armani where she worked closely with him. She went on to establish her award-winning consultancy, Yulan Creative. She has now twenty-five years experience working with renowned UK heritage and international brands. Over the last seven years she has also worked to grow ecommerce fashion businesses, one of which quadrupled its turnover in only three years. Another, in less than a year from launch, won multiple awards and accolades from YOOX, *Vogue Italy* and Anna Wintour.

Whether working with multi-billion corporations or growing SMEs, Joanne's winning combination of high-level creative vision and entrepreneurship has consistently created breakthrough business for clients.

Joanne regularly lectures and speaks on the fashion business. Her unique blend of mentoring workshops and implementation helps owner led creative businesses *align* their creative and business strategies and stand out in a very competitive market.

Made in the USA
Middletown, DE
21 December 2019